KEIO MONOGRAPHS OF BUSINESS AND COMMERCE

I

Essays in the Theory of Wages and Prices

by

RYOICHI SUZUKI

Professor of Econometrics

SOCIETY OF BUSINESS AND COMMERCE,
KEIO UNIVERSITY, TOKYO JAPAN

1967

Printed by The Keio Tsushin Co. Ltd.,
Mita Tsunamachi 1, Minatoku, Tokyo, Japan

Preface

This is a compilation of my articles I have publicated in English up to the present since the days of my visit for study to University of California in 1961.

Contrastively to the so-called latent unemployment from which the Japanese economy had long been suffering, after the business boom in and around 1960 problems of new phase have been at the front; wage increases in, inter alia, medium-small scale enterprises due to the labor shortage resulting from expanded job opportunities and, at the same time, rises in consumer prices. As an underlying fact in these situations, in Chapter 1, I have pointed out that the real wages in pre-boom Japan, in comparison with international levels, were relatively higher than the nominal wages, because the consumer prices of those days were held cheap relatively to the yen exchange-rate.

In Chapter 2, I have tried to set forth a theoretical definition of the rise in price. By the traditional theory on price-index, price changes are followed up with respect to each category of goods, being specified, and any case of shift in demand toward superior goods is counted as a level-up in the standard of living, not a rise in the price. Under the condition of a growth-economy, however, it should be non-sense to select "a person having the same amount of income for the compared period as that for the basic period" as the typical man. It seems to be more reasonable instead to take a person whose income increases at an equal rate with the growth of the national economy" as such one. Hence, it may be proper to introduce, as regards the standard of utility also, the "relative income hypothesis" which assumes that, due to demonstration effect, purchases of inferior goods will decline following a rise in the income level of the entire society. I have intended to adapt this theory to the calculation of price-index and studied out a new formula for it.

Chapter 3 is devoted to some observations on the differentials, between Japan and America, in the wages-productivity-employment structures as seen in the data by median-grouping of industries. In Chapter 4, a supplement to the preceding chapter, I have made a suggestion for amending the defects involved in the customary formula of computing indexes of productivity and wages. This chapter is reproduced from the Productivity Review, Organization for Economic Cooperation and Development, August 1963.

In Chapter 5, I have examined by medium of Cobb-Douglas function, how an increase in productivity owing to innovation will exert effect upon the distributive shares of wages and profit, and further gone into verifying that the theoretical value of income-inequality coefficient is larger than the theoretical value of Gini's index of concentration and smaller than the transformed value of Pareto constant.

Chapter 6 shows the results of my measurements on the correlations between changes in consumer prices and those in productivity, wages and growth rate, relying upon data for Japan, America, Britain, West Germany and Italy. The results seem to suggest that the demand-pull theory has wider applicability than the cost-push theory.

As readers will see in the above introduction, essays in this book have been devoted to theoretical as well as positive analyses of fluctuations in productivity, wages and prices, Chapter 1 was once typewritten as an unpublished paper of University of California. I should like to express my gratitude to the university and to the OECD for kindly giving me the permission for reproducing in this volume.

March 1967

Ryoichi Suzuki

CONTENTS

III. Concluding Remarks
    Bibliography

CHAPTER 1.

AN INTERNATIONAL COMPARISON OF THE STANDARD OF LIVING

I. Introduction

An international comparison of the standard of living in ten countries will be discussed with the aid of two empirical methods: first, cross-section analysis for a single year, and second, time-series analysis of the rate of growth of per capita income.

The term, "standard of living," is defined as the total utility enjoyed by the population of each country. In this paper per capita income is substituted as a measure of total utility, which is not measurable; this substitution raises two questions.

First, how should the utility of savings be measured? Time-preference theory defines savings as future consumption. The utility of savings can then be counted as discounted utility. However, in the process of capital accumulation, not all saving is carried on for future consumption; some saving is carried on in order to accumulate liquid assets and obtain a stream of income from these assets.

Second, how can a measure of the disutility of labor be reconciled with the existing national income figure? If Pigou's First Theorem in *Welfare Economics* is to be satisfied, the total utility of each worker is always larger than the disutility of labor. Per capita income could be treated as an index number of welfare, but in order to do so, we will have to assume that the supply of labor is an increasing function of the real wage. If this assumption is not made, the poorer citizens of a country will supply more labor than

the wealthier citizens.   Under such conditions the disutility of labor
will not be equal to labor supply and the lower income groups will
receive the smaller welfare as is described in Pigou's Theorem.
Welfare differentials among workers will then exceed income differentials.

Despite the two questions raised by the use of per capita income
as a measure of utility, per capita real income will be used as a
first approximation of the standard of living in this study.

Exchange rates are often used in comparing income levels.   However, exchange rates do not always coincide with relative costs of
living.   The relative price of the same articles may be different in
each country even with free trade.   In the United States producers'
goods and durable goods are relatively cheap as compared to the
cost of services.   In Japan, on the other hand, the price for services
is relatively cheap when compared with the cost of durable goods.
Television sets sell for $150 to $180, and short-haul bus rides are
four to five cents.   The cost of living in Japan is then really less
than is indicated by the exchange rate of $1.00=¥360.

In order to compare real income levels it is necessary to calculate,
with the use of cross-section data, a real index of the cost of living
for each country.   Irving Fisher's Ideal Formula for cross-section
data can be used, but conventionally it is a laborious process.   For-
tunately, Colin Clark has computed a real index number for the cost
of living for the years 1929 and 1930.   Time series data have been
used to compare his figures with the cost of living in 1957.

1957 was chosen because governments after World War II con-
trolled their foreign trade.   Under these conditions the exchange
rate between countries did not always coincide with the price ratio.
But by 1957 government controls had been considerably removed.

Changes in the real cost of living between the years 1929 and
1957 were measured in the following manner.   A cost-of-living index
for each country was used to calculate the change in real price
ratios between the United States and each country.   This figure
was then compared to the change in exchange rates from 1927 to
1957.   If the change in the price ratio exceeded the change in the
rate of exchange, the real cost of living was considered to be greater

in 1957 than it was in 1929. The change in the real price ratio, based on an equilibrium definition of purchasing power, was then divided by the change in the exchange rate. Finally, the result was multiplied by Colin Clark's real index number to yield the real ratio for the cost of living for 1957.

This method raises a question concerning cost-of-living indexes. In many countries the cost-of-living index is calculated by the Laspeyres' Formula. Haberler has pointed out that the Laspeyres' Formula has an upward bias when compared to the theoretical value of the cost of living. When the cost of living rises by the same amount in each country, this bias is neutralized, but this has not been the actual situation. Increases in the cost of living for different countries are not comparable. Larger increases in the cost of living may be said to contain a larger bias when compared to the theoretical value of the cost of living.

Price indexes for ten countries were obtained in the following manner:

1. *Japan.* The Consumers Price Index for Japan has been computed, since 1930, by the Economic Planning Agency. The C.P.I. is based on urban dwellers' purchases, as in many other countries, and omits rural population.

2. *United States.* The base year of the Consumers Price Index was changed to the year used by L. R. Klein in *Economic Fluctuations in the United States.* For the years since 1935 the Bureau of Labor Statistics C.P.I. has been adjusted to Klein's figures.

3. *United Kingdom.* Colin Clark's cost-of-living data for the years 1920 to 1939 were used. Index numbers of retail prices for the years 1934, 1946, and 1953 were available, which I then related to the 1929 base.

4. *France.* For the period before 1935 Colin Clark's data were also used. The French Government has published three different retail price indexes. These were combined with Clark's data to yield a 1929 base.

5. *Italy.* Two price indexes with base years 1930 and 1953 were used for a new 1951 base and then related to 1929.

6. Continuous indexes based on 1929 were obtained for Switzer-

land, Sweden, Holland, Australia, and Canada in the same manner. Time-series figures were not available for Germany, Austria, and New Zealand.

Exchange rates were available for most of the countries studied. The banking exchange rate was used for Switzerland and the selling exchange rate for Canada.

Per capita income in this paper is defined as total income divided by total population. This definition contrasts with Colin Clark's definition of per capita income as total income divided by the labor force.

II. Per Capita Income and Purchasing Power

The three tables in this section provide the basis for our comparison of levels of living.

Table I. Real Ratio of Purchasing Power [a]

United States	1.00	Switzerland	1.173
United Kingdom	0.784	Australia	0.912
Japan	0.612 [b] (0.758) [c]	Canada	0.847
France	1.00	Sweden	0.990
Italy	1.105	Holland	0.740

a) Ratio of the cost-of-living index divided by the rate of change of the exchange rate.
b) Computed by indirect method.
c) Computed by direct method.

Where the figure exceeds the base of 1.00, the purchasing power in that country is higher than indicated by the exchange rate. For example, the consumer's real purchasing power in Japan is 360× 0.612 or 220 yen.

Since the definition used in this paper of per capita income is different from the one used by Colin Clark, his figures and these are not comparable. However, in those cases where the ratio of total labor force to total population is unchanged, his findings and these may be compared as a first approximation.

Colin Clark, using Irving Fisher's Ideal Formula, calculated

Table II.   Per Capita Income Adjusted for Real Purchasing Power
for the Year 1957 (in dollar)

Japan	412 a) (332) b)	Sweden	1,282
United States	2,225	Holland	932
United Kingdom	1,175	Italy	365
France	846	Canada	1,722
Switzerland	1,055	Australia	1,192

a)   Computed by indirect method.
b)   Computed by direct method.

the real purchasing power for Japan as 0.758.   But even when
Fisher's Formula is used, a comparison between the United States
and Japan could not be directly arrived at because of differences
in the items and weights used in the consumers price indexes of
the two countries.   Instead, the chain index method had to be
used.   The United States was compared to the United Kingdom
and then the United Kingdom to Japan.   Finally, the United
States was related to Japan.

Calculation errors may enter into this process, perhaps caused
by the time insert test.   If we divide our own estimates of real
per capita income by the normal income ratio, a different price
ratio, 0.612, is obtained for Japan than the one cited by Clark.

Theoretically, Clark's results appear to be better.   However,
from my examination of the time-series information, I believe the
results obtained by the second method to be more realistic.

The growth rate of the real per capita income in Table II with
Colin Clark's figures is presented in Table III.   The growth rate
for Sweden between 1929 and 1957 is 282% assuming that the
ratio of total labor force to total population is .50.   The rates of
growth for other countries examined are:

Table III.   Growth in Per Capita Income, 1929-1957

Canada	157%	United Kingdom	120 %
France	147%	Holland	118 %
Australia	143%	Switzerland	107.6%
Japan	134%	Italy	107.0%
United States	132%		

From Table III we may infer the following:

1. The United States enjoyed the highest per capita income before and after World War II.

2. Sweden shows the greatest rate of growth, exceeding all other countries examined. Is this because Sweden did not participate in World War II?

3. Switzerland, a country that did not join in World War II, shows a very low rate of growth. From this we may conclude that nonparticipation in war is not a significant factor in determining a country's growth of per capita income.

4. The United Kingdom ranked third in per capita income before World War II but fell, after the war, to fifth. Perhaps this was due to her losses during the war.

5. The high rate of growth of the Japanese economy has often been explained by the fact that Japan suffered great losses during the war. In the process of trying to recover her prewar standards, the country suceeded in raising its rate of growth. Figures indicate that the income level of Japan for 1946–1947 was about a third less than the prewar level. Thus the country has not had as high a rate of growth as is assumed if the average rate of growth from 1930 to 1957 is examined.

6. Italy showed the lowest rate of growth of per capita income before and after World War II. The importance of the new figures presented above can be demonstrated by comparing Italy with Japan.

If per capita income is used to compare the two countries, without consideration of the differences in price, income level in Japan is lower than that of Italy. If the real income level is used, Japan's per capita income is higher than Italy's, and this new figure then places Italy at the bottom of the ranking.

It can be concluded that there is no correlation between income level and rate of growth. The rate of growth of the United States and Japan is almost the same, whereas there are large differences in per capita income. See Table III. Ranking of countries according to rate of growth will result in a much different order than ranking by per capita income.

Dynamic analysis, not static observations, must be used to explain rates of growth, particularly in analyzing the relationship between savings and investment.

III. The Effect of Economic Planning

After World War II many governments established economic planning commissions in an effort to recover prewar standards of living. As a part of economic planning, "projections" of future national income were made. A striking fact about these "projections" was that the realized value of national income often exceeded the projected value. What was different about the postwar period?

The investment-national income ratio after World War II was larger than before the war. There are two possible reasons for this. First, after the destruction caused by the war, new investment and new construction occurred which exceeded the prewar situation. Second, governments, in making economic projections, attempted to avoid depression, such as occurred in 1929, and in trying to decrease the possibility of panic encouraged investment.

A second characteristic of the postwar situation was the decrease in the capital coefficient ratio. In Japan, this coefficient was estimated at about 5.00 in 1930. However, by 1955 the marginal capital coefficient ratio had decreased to about 3.00. If investment had continued at the same level after the war, the national income produced by that investment would have been larger in the postwar period.

Another possible reason for the underestimation of national income was the overestimation of capital-output ratios. The postwar inflationary gap in many countries made people desire savings. At the time Keynes wrote, 1930–1936, savings exceeded investment and the question of disposable excess savings was important. But after World War II there was a need to save.

Consumption in the postwar period was examined by the use of government data. Four countries were surveyed: the United States, a high level-of-income country; Sweden, a high rate-of-growth country; Italy, a low level-of-income and low rate-of-growth country; and Japan.

Private consumption and government consumption should be used in calculating the propensity to consume, but only private consumption was examined, since many countries do not distinguish between consumption and investment in their classification of government expenditures.

The time-lag relationship should be clarified in analyzing capital formation and the real value of income and savings should be compared. Sweden and Italy had no appropriate deflator, and so the relationship between nominal national income and savings was used. The following consumption patterns occurred after World War II.

1. *Japan.* Consumption exceeded national income in the years 1946, 1947, and 1948 because of a sharp drop in per capita income. In 1949 there was a turning point in the effectiveness of the Dodge Plan, and the propensity to consume slowly decreased. In the years 1954–1955 the propensity to consume rose slightly, but this was an exception to the trend.

2. *United States.* The propensity to consume was low in the period 1947–1950, except for 1949. Since 1953, with the exception of 1956, the propensity to consume has been high and there has been an inflationary tendency in the economy.

3. *Italy.* The propensity to consume has been high, when compared to the other countries examined, particularly for the years 1948, 1949 and 1952.

4. *Sweden.* The propensity to consume has been relatively low throughout the postwar period.

The data examined covered only the postwar period and it is not possible to draw any general conclusions. However, an examination of four countries may serve as partial proof for the theorem that a high propensity to save is a necessary condition for the maintenance of a high rate of growth. This theorem was presented by Roy F. Harrod in *Towards a Dynamic Economics.*

While a high propensity to save may raise the standard of living in the future, continuous increases in savings may decrease the utility derived from current consumption.   Several economists after Keynes have treated savings as the residual, reduced consumption from current income.   Is this an appropriate treatment?   It is necessary to examine the future satisfaction derived from current savings in order to deal with questions about the rate of growth.

IV. The Changes of Real Wages

What effect does labor's share of the national income have on a nation's level of living?

Wages of manufacturing workers were used in the analysis of the relative share of the national income going to labor.   This is consistent with our use of cost-of-living data which are based on the urban population.   The index number for time series data could not be used in a comparison of wage levels among countries without tying the index number to absolute value.

In the analysis of labor's share, the usual question arose of whether to use hourly wages or weekly wages.   If the weekly wages are used, even though they fit neatly into an analysis of the standard of living, different labor conditions can bias the conclusions.   Through the use of hourly wages, quantitative differences in labor can be eliminated although the qualitative problem remains.

Six countries were considered: the United States, the United Kingdom, Japan,[1] Canada, Australia,[2] and France.

The real hourly wage for each country was computed by the same method as real income.   See Section II.   Real hourly wages were compared with real per capita income for each country, and it was necessary to compute the per capita income for the labor force.   Unfortunately, it was not possitble to get labor force figures for all countries, and per capita income for the entire population had to be used.   See Table IV.

---

1)   Only monthly wage data were available.   The hourly wage was computed by dividing the monthly wage by the average number of hours worked per month.
2)   1956 data were used.

1. In the United States the real wage level in 1949 exceeded
the real wage level of 1937 by about 24%. Despite the comparatively low rate of growth, the real wage rose during the post-
World War II period. This may have some relation to the low
rate of growth of the national income.

2. The United Kingdom ranks fourth in per capita income but
its wage level exceeds Australia and approximates that of Canada.
The difference in wage levels between the United States and the
United Kingdom is smaller than the difference in per capita income between the two countries.

   The change in real wages has been similar to that of the United
States but, unlike the United States, real national income during
World War II decreased in the United Kingdom. It is possible
that there was a shift in the distribution of income among industries and a shift in the relative share going to labor.

3. In Japan, at the end of the war, labor productivity and real
wages fell to a low level, because of the almost total destruction
of industrial equipment. In 1949 the real wage was about 60%
of the 1935 real wage. From 1949 the wage level rose rapidly
and by 1952 the wage level had exceeded the prewar level. The
real wage level continued to rise after 1955, although the rate of
growth fell slightly.

4. Real wages in Canada have changed similarly to real wages
in the United States.

5. Although only hourly wage data are available for Australia,
they indicate that, since 1950, the wage level has been relatively
constant. Real per capita income exceeds that of the United Kingdom, but real wages are slightly lower.

6. France, from 1950 to 1957, experienced a high rate of
growth of real wages, exceeding that of Japan. However, in
1958, a turning point was reached and the real wage since then
has decreased. At present, the wage level in France is very low
when compared with the income level.

   How can the differences between wage levels and income levels
be explained?

   Economists often explain differences in wages by differences in labor productivity. But this tells us nothing about why differences in labor productivity occur.

Differences in labor productivity may be the result of differences in the industrial structure of countries. But one must ask, is there some other variable that can better explain the differential? In order to answer this question it would be necessary to compare the per capita income levels of workers engaged in "secondary industries," as defined by Colin Clark.

Another explanation for the differences in wage levels is the dissimilarity in the unemployment ratio among countries. The relative share going to labor is usually computed including the unemployed members of the labor force. Knowledge of a nation's unemployment figures is necessary for a more realistic picture of per capita wage data.

Differences in labor supply may also account for the differences between hourly wages and per capita wages in a country. This factor will be discussed in the next section.

V. Wage Differentials

What effect do wage differentials and labor supply have on real income and real wages?

Cross-section data for eight countries were used to obtain the correlation between real wages and hours worked per week.[3]

The eight countries examined were: Japan, the United States, the United Kingdom, France, Canada, Australia, Switzerland and Italy. See Table V. With such a small sample size it is difficult to generalize about whether the correlation between real wages and hours worked is positive or negative. From Table V the United Kingdom is the only country that may have a negative correlation.

There is a problem of the identification of the curve. Does the

3)   For Japan, hours per week were not available, and hours worked per month were used. The hours worked per week were computed by multiplying the result of 7/30.4 by the hours worked per month. 30.4 is the result of 365/12, or the average days per month.

computed regression line indicate the demand curve for labor or the supply curve for labor? This regression line is not a "schedule" but the "observed" values.

Even if the Marshall-Pigou theorem of the disutility of labor is assumed, labor supply does not always increase with increases in real wages. In the United States, Canada, and Australia the real wage is high but the average working days short. These three countries suffer from a shortage of labor and there is a strong tendency towards wage inflation.

In 1956 the hourly wage was low, and the hours worked high, in Japan, Italy and Switzerland. In Italy, the proportion of unemployed to the total population was large. In Japan, although the proportion of unemployed was relatively small, there was a great deal of potential unemployment.

A shortage labor does not explain the short working days in developed countries. In the United States, Canada, and Australia the demand for labor is high. Is it possible to state that the negative correlation between real wages and hours worked has been determined by the behavior of the labor supply? This question is asked because demand does not appear to explain the differences between real income and real wages.

An analysis of family income and expenditures yielded information about the behavior of the labor supply curve. From this data it can be concluded that the correlation between real wages and hours worked cannot be explained by Classical theory. The supply of labor is not an explicity increasing function of the real wage. Classical theory does not apply, because the supply of labor is not divisible. Where trade unions are strong, the hours of work have been shortened, but in other situations few people will voluntarily work 25 hours a week. The most frequent choice before the laborer is whether he will work more than 40 hours a week, or not work at all.

Another reason why the supply of labor is not an increasing function of the real wage is that the laborer must feed not only himself, but a family. The wife may work or stay at home, depending upon what her husband's paycheck is. Similarly, whether a young man or woman enters college or goes to work depends on the earnings of the principal family worker. For these two reasons, the labor supply may be negatively correlated with real wages.

It is possible that in underdeveloped countries the labor supply is large because wages are so low.

Can the marginal utility received from each worker's wage be compared for different countries? The disutility of labor supply raises similar questions. In the developed countries a wide range of wants is affected by the "demonstration effect."

In any consideration of the standard of living it is necessary to examine the distribution of income in addition to the average level of wages. This must be done when we compare the utility of different peoples.

For the long-run situation Pigou, in *The Economics of Welfare*, has stated the homogeneous utility function that can be used in making comparisons. It takes into consideration the possibility

Table IV.

Country	(A) Cost of Living[a] 1957	(B) Cost of Living in Relationship to the U.S.	(C) Cost of Living 1929	(D) Change in Exchange Rates in Relationship to the U.S.	(E) B/D
United States	1.627	1.000	1.000	1.000	1.000
United Kingdom	2.590	1.590	0.854	1.735	0.916
Japan	305.000	182.500	0.606[b] 0.750[c]	180.000	1.010
France	36.700	22.500	0.730	16.450	1.365
Italy	64.000	38.200	0.948	32.800	1.165
Switzerland	1.540	0.923	1.045	0.825	1.120
Australia	2.315	1.385	1.149	1.770	0.783
Canada	1.568	0.940	0.888	0.985	0.953
Sweden	2.300	1.375	0.997	1.385	0.993
Holland	2.550	1.528	0.740	1.530	1.000

a) 1929 base.
b) Computed by indirect method.
c) Computed by direct method.

Table IV. (Continued)

Country	(F) (C)×(E)	(G) Income Per Member[d]) of the Labor Force 1929-1934	(H) Per Capita Income[d]) in Dollars 1957	(I) Hourly Wages[d]) 1956	(J) Hours Worked per Week
United States	1.000	1,381	2,225	1.980	40.0
United Kingdom	0.784	1,069	1,175	1.850	46.0
Japan	0.612[b]) 0.758[c])	353	412[b]) 332[c])	0.397	47.7
France	1.000	684	846	0.436	45.4
Italy	1.105	343	365	0.282	49.2
Switzerland	1.173	1,018	1,055	0.649	47.7
Australia	0.912	980	1,192	1.730	40.0
Canada	0.847	1,337	1,722	1.855	41.1
Sweden	0.990	653	1,282	0.746	e)
Holland	0.740	855	932	e)	e)

d) In terms of Colin Clark's international unit.
e) No figure available.

Table V. Index of Real Wages[a])

Year	Japan	United States	United Kingdom	France	Canada	Australia
1937	93.5	62	56.4[b])	c)	65.5	77
1949	62.0	86	101.0	84.0	86.0	94
1950	80.9	92	101.0	83.0	88.0	98
1951	86.0	93	99.0	90.0	89.0	98
1952	95.0	96	99.0	90.0	89.0	98
1953	100.0	100	100.0	100.0	100.0	100
1954	99.0	107	102.0	105.0	101.0	101
1955	104.0	107	105.0	112.0	105.0	101
1956	113.0	110	108.0	123.0	109.0	99
1957	114.0	109	109.0	130.0	c)	100
1958	117.0	108	110.0	124.0	110.0	100

a) 1953 base.
b) 1938 figure used.
c) No figure available.

of adaptation to new circumstances and widens the area of choice for those considering entrance into the labor market.

If this reasoning is valid for underdeveloped countries, the marginal disutility of labor may exceed the marginal utility of wages at the point where the wage is determined.

CHAPTER 2.

COST OF LIVING INDEX UNDER RAPID ECONOMIC GROWTH

I. *Introduction*

In this paper it will be discussed that under a rapid income growth conventional type of cost of living index could not describe increasing (or decreasing) standard of living on the theoretical view point. Changing price system compels a consumer to adjust to it quickly, though his reaction speed is not so rapid as relative-price changes. Moreover growth of income is not even among consumers: someone enjoys higher increase in income, while the other bothers less increase in income. Recent studies on consumer behavior suggest the mutual-dependence of consumer preference. It is, therefore, supposed that differential increase in income would perhaps have any influences other than expected in traditional treatment of the problem.

Professor Haberler [1] proved, assuming the constancy of consumer preference, (1) the Laspeyres' price index is the upper limit of price average in equilibrium and (2) the Paasche price index is the lower limit of price average in equilibrium, where the "price average" means price index weighted by the equilibrium quantities which give the same utility as before. This proposition shows that, even though assuming *constant preference* and *same utility level,* either conventional formula will over- or understate the true picture and bring invalid measurement of cost of living.

II. Changes in Prices and Delayed Consumer Response

Our first point to be discussed is as follows. Even if the consumer preference is unchanged, when the price system has changed very rapidly, consumer adjustment will be delayed by his psychological immobility. In other words lags will be observed in consumer's response to price changes. In a usual growth process technological innovation will push down the prices of consumer durables, and in turn the prices of service goods will be increased or, at least, increased by innovation.

Consequently relative prices of services will be risen up. Such a sudden rise in price of service goods will not be immediately followed by decrease in demand for it. People will continue to buy and use the services in the following times and then the demand will at least be expected to decrease gradually. For example people, who is accustomed to use taxi service, would continue to follow his original behavioristic pattern instead of choosing own driving. Substitution by automobile might occur after some time had passed. In this circumstance usual price indices probably could not describe consumer's impression on rising prices. He would urge the price index to be re-computed up to the level that he feels. When the price index increases by 10%, the variance of prices will be considerably great each other. I believe, it is appropriate to use any modified formula in these situations. Specifically standard deviation of prices (or individual price indices) should be added to our usual price index. As an illustrative example is calculated: our consumer price index

(Laspeyres' formula, P_{01}^{L}, in 1962 is 112.2 as compared to 1960

while the proposal one, i.e. $\overline{P}_{01}^{L} = P_{01}^{L} + \sigma_p$, becomes 117.1, where

$\sigma_p = 4.9$ is standard deviation of prices in 1962, that is $\sum \left[\left(p_1^i - \tilde{p}_1 \right) \right.$

$\left. \cdot \left(p_0^i \quad q_0^i \right) \right]$. In general, the coefficient of σ_p needs not be unity, and

may be any constant equal to change in marginal utility of money
if could have been measured.

III. Demonstration Effect and New Index

In his celebrated study of consumer behavior Professor Duesenberry [2] discussed the mutual-dependence of consumer prefer-
ences in a community. If we accept the hypothesis, and also do
not ignore the differential rate of income growth among consumers
(or some consumer groups,) our cost of living index may be con-
verted to the ones described below:

$$(2.1) \qquad P_{01}^{L} = \sum p_1 q_0 \frac{Q_1}{q_1} \frac{q_0}{Q_0} \div \sum p_0 q_0$$

$$(2.2) \qquad P_{01}^{P} = \sum p_1 q_1 \div \sum p_0 q_1 \frac{q_1}{Q_1} \frac{Q_0}{q_0}$$

Where p_0 and p_1 stand for prices in base year and comparative
year respectively, and q's denote the purchased quantities of consumers goods in any specific consumer group, while Q's mean the
aggregates of q's, i.e., consumption of each commodities in economy at large. The suffix 0 and 1 to both q and Q are the same
as to p's. Our new index, either the Laspeyres' or the Passche's
type, which were expected to include the existence of demonstration effect in consumer behavior, is different in its weighting
quantity when compared to usual ones. In usual the (change in)
prices are weighted by the *absolute* quantities of corresponding commodities, only while in our proposed one the *relative* quantities are
used. In consequence we have so many numbers of price index as
any consumer groups that are homogenous in each group and hetero-
geneous among them. For the consumer whose monthly earning
is between 15 and 20 thousand yen in 1960, new price index in
1962 is computed as 110.1. However the monthly expenditure of
average working class in selected big cities has increased from
¥30,137 in 1960 to ¥37,010 in 1962, that is, grown up by 22.8%
The consumer specified above, whose income grew up less than the
average consumer, would feel price increase more seriously.

IV. New Index and Haberler's Proposition

The above indices (1) and (2) could not pass the familiar tests,
that is, factor reversal and time reversal tests and so on. But if
we combine them, they can pass those tests. Let us write welfare
indices correspondingly:

$$(2.3) \qquad W_{01}^{L} = \frac{\sum p_0 q_1 \dfrac{q_1}{Q_1} \cdot \dfrac{Q_0}{q_0}}{\sum p_0 q_0}$$

$$(2.4) \qquad W_{01}^{P} = \sum p_1 q_1 \Big/ \sum p_1 q_0 \frac{Q_1}{q_1} \cdot \frac{q_0}{Q_0}$$

Then we have (: factor reversal test),

$$P_{01}^{L} \times W_{01}^{P} = \frac{\sum p_1 q_1}{\sum p_0 q_0}$$

And also we have (: time reversal test),

$$P_{01}^{L} \times P_{10}^{P} = 1$$

In this context, however, our indices do not coincide with theoretical price index which is derived from any appropriate indif-
ference maps. According to an analogous reasoning as Haberler's, we may reach the similar conclusion about the relationships
between new indices and theoretical index as was summarized
above. It should be noted here that if habit formation of consumer behavior took place so rapidly, the equal utility presumption
could hardly be supported. Our discussions, therefore, should
be valid if and only if consumer's habit might have any lagged
effects on future consumptions.

V. Aggregation and Social Welfare

Our index, thus constructed for every consumer group, should
be aggregated to the one for the whole consumers. For simpli-
city let us suppose that the (changes in) distribution of income
could be approximately well described by a simple statistic λ,
coefficient of inequality. Let denote the inequality in any comparative year as λ_1. Our social price index, or cost of living,

would be.

$$(2.5) \qquad P_{01}(\lambda_1/\lambda_0) = P_{01}\left(1 + \frac{\varDelta\lambda_1}{\lambda_0}\right),$$

where $\lambda_1 = \lambda_0 + \varDelta\lambda_1$. This formula suggests that social cost of living would be higher as social income is more unequally distributed. In other words it may be considered that the consumer with less increased income would perhaps feel the rising price more seriously than the other with more increased income.

The other base discussed in Chapter 5 that in a developing economy the relation (2.6) tends to be held:

$$(2.6) \qquad \alpha/\alpha - 1 \geq \lambda \geq \delta$$

where λ, α and δ are inequality coefficients of Lorenz., Pareto and Gini distribution. If (2.6) is to be accepted, the theoretical cost of living for whole consumer, denoted by I_{01}, may be between $P_{01}^{L}\left(\dfrac{\alpha}{\alpha-1}\right)$ and $P_{01}^{P}\delta$, where P_{01}^{L} and P_{01}^{P} are respectively our new indices, Laspeyres' and Paasche type, for the consumer group with average income. This relation sets up the upper and lower limits of our cost of living for the economy as a whole.

BIBLIOGRAPHY

1   Gottfried Haberler, *Der Sinn der Indexzahlen*, 1927
2   James Duesenberry, *Income, Saving and Consumer Behavior*, 1953

CHAPTER 3.

AN INTERNATIONAL COMPARISON OF THE WAGE STRUCTURE AND EMPLOYMENT IN THE MANUFACTURING INDUSTRY

I. Introduction

In this chapter we will be engaged in a rather detailed international comparison of wage levels in the manufacturing industry, with special emphasis on the difference between the United States and Japan.

It should be observed in the first place that the major factor which brings forth wage differences between any two countries is the difference in wage structures among various manufacturing industries, as described in the previous chapter.

In Japan, the high rate of growth of the national income after the war has been called a "splendid" accomplishment. The real wages have also shown a rapid rate of increase during the same period. It is to be noted, however, that the annual rate of growth in real wages has not been invariable from one period to another. Between 1946 and 1952, the real wages in manufacturing industry increased with a speed which approximately paralleled, or slightly exceeded, the rate of increase in labor productivity; whereas, after 1953, the growth rate of real wages has been lower than that of labor productivity. (The labor productivity is measured in terms of the aggregate sum of products divided by the number of laborers.)

We may suggest the following as the dominant factor for explaining this phenomenon.

The employment in the manufacturing industry increased during the war, especially in heavy and chemical industries. After the war, owing to war damages, the production of manufacturing industry was on an extremely low level, which caused the number of employees to exceed the number of workers who were actually needed for maintaining the current production level. This created a great amount of "latent" unemployment, i.e., the people who were not actually engaged in production, but still remained in firms as "nominal" employees. As production increased, of course, the "latent" unemployment gradually disappeared. This made it necessary for a firm to increase employment in order to increase the production level. Real wages in manufacturing industry restored its prewar level in 1952. Nevertheless, the unemployment in the society as a whole did not yet completely disappear. The supply of labor continued to exceed the demand, and this was the primary reason why real wages failed to reach a higher level in proportion to higher productivity of labor.

Since 1959, however, the situation has changed completely. Owing to the increase in production level, unemployed youths have disappeared. The demand for labor has exceeded the supply of labor, and it has become increasingly difficult to expand production because of the labor shortage. After 1961, the tendency of cost inflation has been detected. Small firms have particularly suffered for lack of labor. Real wages now have a tendency to rise in comparison with the price of producers' goods. On the other hand, the "consumption revolution" is now under way due to the increase in real income. This accounts for the rising trend in the prices of several consumer goods.

The Japanese government has been planning to double the real national income during the next ten years. However, in the light of the recent price movement, we must say that it is a very regrettable defect of this plan that the change in relative prices is not taken into consideration.

One of the advantages of international comparison is that we can make use of the experiences in more developed economies in forecasting the most likely future of the relevant economy in consideration, thus eliminating the unavoidable uncertainties which are involved in a long-term economic prediction. The pattern of price structure in Japan seems to be approaching that of the Western countries. Because of the difference in distribution of resources, it is improbable that the Japanese price structure will become exactly the same as that in the Western European countries. For example, the absolute limitation of the area will never allow the number of automobiles in Japan to increase as much as that in the United States, even if the per capita income were raised, say, by five times the current income level. In spite of this difficulty, however, we will compare the wage and employment structures of the United States and Japan, in order to forecast, as a first approximation, the future condition of the Japanese economy.

II. The Effects of Economic Development upon the Prices and Wage Rates

In doing international comparison of economic conditions between two or more countries, we may observe the following facts:

(1) In more developed countries, on account of a higher degree of capital accumulation, the price of producers' goods is relatively cheaper and the price of services higher, than in less developed countries.

(2) In more developed countries, the relative shortage of labor causes real wages to be higher and the relative share of labor comparatively greater, than in less advanced nations. After World War II, the relative share increased about sixty-five per cent in the United States, approximately sixty per cent in the United Kingdom, and about fifty per cent in France. In Japan, on the other hand, it fell down to as low as thirty per cent in 1946. As the production level rose again, however, the relative share increased as well and exceeded fifty per cent in 1956. It should be noted also that the relative share of labor tends to increase gradually over time.

(3) There seems to be no close relationship between the rate of growth of national income and the changes in wage rates.

(4)   There is a negative correlation between real wages and working hours per week.

Now we can go into the comparison of the wage and employment structures in manufacturing industry between the United States and Japan.   The original data for the United States were taken from *Employment and Earnings,* edited by the U. S. Department of Labor.   As for the Japanese data, we have used the *Labor Statistics 1959,* edited by the Japanese Ministry of Labor.   We shall confine our investigation to the comparison of wages of production workers.   We shall also deal only with the wages per head and exclude the hourly wage rates from our consideration due to the lack of data.

In dealing with the Japanese wage statistics, we have to take account of special items such as allowances paid in kind, bonuses, and retirement pensions which occupy a large proportion of the earnings of a Japanese laborer.   In other words, the difference in wages (per head) between the United States and Japan will be overestimated, unless we take heed to this fact.   Unfortunately, however, it is very difficult to ascertain numerically the roles of these items because of limited data.   In particular, the estimated value of allowance in kind will be vastly different according to whether we compute it on the basis of market price or the costs borne by firms.   Consequently, we are forced to compare the unadjusted money-wage rates between these countries as a first approximation.

Ideally, we should compare the wages specified according to ages, occupation, education, sex, and the length of service.   In other words, we should compare the wages of a similar nature, so far as it is possible.   In the present study, however, this procedure was not followed, simply because it would diminish the sample size to such a degree that the comparison becomes insignificant.   For this reason, we will restrict ourselves to the comparison of the average wage levels in the classified manufacturing industries.

To eliminate bonuses from the Japanese wage statistics, it was considered appropriate to pick up the month which normally does not coincide with the one for payment of such enumeration. Thus the data for September (1959) were chosen for our purpose of study (see Table I).

There are two more things to be mentioned concerning the nature of the data. First, in order to convert the wages in the United States industries to the Japanese standard (yen), we will assume that the exchange rate is $1 to ¥300, although, as described in the previous chapter, it seems that the purchasing power of the Japanese currency is even stronger than this exchange rate. Second, it is to be noted that the wages in the United States are on the weekly basis, whereas in Japan they are paid by month. Therefore, we have converted the American wage figures into the monthly basis by multiplying them by 30/7. This is roughly the procedure by which we acquired the wage figures and the number of laborers in each manufacturing industry.

III. The Industrial Structure of U.S.A. and Japan

In analyzing the statistical figures in both countries, we may make the following two remarks:

(1)   Since the total population of the United States is larger than that of Japan, and the former is more developed in industrialization than the latter, the number of employees in each manufacturing industry in the United States is larger than that of Japan in absolute number. This is rightly so. Observing the proportion of each industry in detail, however, one will notice that the proportion of employment in the finished-good industries in the United States is larger than that in Japan and conversely with the raw-material industry. A few examples of the former industries are: textile, coal and petroleum product, furniture and fixture, and so on. In the latter industrial group, textile-mill product, leather, metal, etc., are included. This fact tells us that the industrial structure in Japan has not yet matured enough to supply finished goods in such a magnitude as is expected in highly industrialized country.

(2)   The wage level in finished-goods industry in the United

States is relatively high compared to that of Japan, and the wage level in raw-material industry comparatively low, with the exception of the tobacco industry. Perhaps this exception is due to the difference in the management system. In Japan, the tobacco industry is run by the government. The circumstantial difference on the demand side thus may have caused the wage difference.

Roughly speaking, the demand for labor in the finished-goods producing industries is relatively high in the United States. But the existence of the greater difference in employment structure between the United States and Japan does not necessarily mean that there is the greater difference in wage structure; and vice versa. For example, the wage rates in the United States, compared with Japan, are the highest in the rubber-product industry; but the (U. S.) employment in this industry is ranked sixteenth. On the other hand, the textile industry is ranked the top in terms of employment, but only fifth in terms of wage difference. This low correlation is perhaps due to the restriction of labor mobility between industries. Furthermore, if we take into account labor productivity as a parameter, we may get a clearer and more satisfactory result.

IV. The Standard of Living of Wage Earners

Next, we will compare the standard of living of wage earners in the United States, Japan, and the United Kingdom.

The figures in Table II are based on the research conducted by the Japanese Ministry of Labor. We will compare the standard of living by using the family-expenditure data. Because the years chosen for the purpose of comparison are different from one country to another and, furthermore, the Japanese data show the monthly earnings, whereas the American data relate to the annual receipt, and the English data to the weekly earnings, it is difficult, strictly speaking, to make a rigorous comparison of the standard of living—although we may still be able to get an overall picture of it.

After these preliminary remarks, the following observations are in order.

(1)   First of all, it should be remembered that our data relate to the receipt before taxation per family unit and, therefore, a direct comparison between the present figures and the wage data is not possible. The mode of the income class in Japan is approximately 22,000 yen, and the number of families which get the income of between 17,000 and 32,000 yen is about eighty-three per cent of the total number of the sample. In the United States, the mode of the family-income class is $3,700 per year, and the number of families that receive the income of between $2,600 and $4,800 is about sixty per cent of the total sample. Therefore, if we compare the family income level not by arithmetic mean but by mode, and use the foreign exchange rate ($1= ¥360) for conversion, the living standard in the United States is about five times higher than that of Japan. Since the years chosen for comparison are different between the countries, we should of course be mindful of the fact that economic growth was taking place during these nine years (i.e., from 1950 to 1959).

The difference of standard of living between the nations estimated in this manner is not so large as that which is computed from the arithmetic mean of the wage data. The first factor which may account for this discrepancy is the different nature of family life.   In Japan, it is customary that individual consumption becomes relevant only in the context of the family expenditure as a whole.   Sometimes in Japan, "family" means a group of two married couples—old and young—and it has been the custom that these two couples live together. The incomes of father and son being summed together, the real family expenditure may take relatively higher value than it would have been otherwise.   Furthermore, the discrepancy may come about depending on whether we employ mode or arithmetic mean. It seems to me that it is better to use mode for the comparison of the standard of living.

In the United Kingdom, the mode is about twelve pounds per week, which corresponds roughly to two or three times as much as the earnings of a Japanese family.

(2)   Secondly, let us observe the balance between receipts and expenditures in a family.

In Japan, the break-even point is at 17,000 yen (per month), which is next below the mode.   If we use the disposable income instead of the receipt before taxation, the break-even point will correspond to a higher income class.   In the United States, on the other hand, the break-even point is at the income class of $3,700, which coincides with the mode-class.   In other words, we can conclude, by comparing the break-even point in these two countries and converting the American income by the foreign exchange rate ($1=¥360), that the American break-even point is approximately six times higher than that of Japan.   How should we interpret this difference?

As Professor Duesenbery explained in his book, *Income, Saving, and Consumer Behavior,* the more advanced the cultural level in a society, the larger becomes the propensity to consume.   In an advanced country, there is a large possibility of being influenced by the "ratchet effect."

The data of the United States are that of 1950.   During the first half of this year, the United States suffered a recession.   As a result, it is conceivable that the propensity to consume in this year became larger than that of a normal or equilibrium year, since the propensity to consume is affected not only by the current level of income, but also by the highest level of income enjoyed by many people in the past—this is the so-called "Modigliani factor."

In addition to this, according to Professor Duesenbery's theory, we should consider the "demonstration effect."   In the United States, the average level of income earned by the majority of people being high, many are stimulated by their neighbors' consumption behavior.   This may lead to an increase in propensity to consume and also in the break-even point.   To add another explanation, there is the "liquid asset theorem."   Owing to the damage caused by the war, the amount of the asset holding of the Japanese family was reduced considerably.   This was probably a factor that lessened the propensity to consume in Japan. If so, we cannot regard the break-even point of these two countries as having been under a reasonably comparable situation. Indeed, it is very difficult to carry out a precise comparison of economic welfare between two or more different countries. It will be the task of the new welfare economics to find the answer to this problem, which may be solved by combining the cross-section analysis and the time-series analysis.

V. Labor Productivity

In the preceding section, we attempted an international comparison of wages and employment in each industry but did not find a close correlation between wage rates and employment. Theoretically, however, these two factors interact each other through the productivity of labor.

According to the wage fund theory, real wages and employment must have a negative correlation, provided that labor productivity is unchanged. But it is of rare occasion that labor productivity remains constant. Therefore, the negative correlation between these two factors is not expected to hold in ordinary circumstances.

In this section, we will analyze the relationship between labor productivity, wage rates, and employment. First, in calculating labor productivity, the question arises whether we should use physical productivity or value productivity. Many students have conventionally used physical productivity. Indeed, if we are analyzing the change of real wages by time-series data, we should calculate productivity in physical terms. But since our purpose here is to compare the nominal wages between two countries, we should calculate value productivity. The reason for this is that the money wages are affected not only by physical productivity but also by the change of market conditions, among which is the change of prices of the final products.

Secondly, we have to face the problem of aggregation, if we stick to physical productivity. Strictly speaking, physical productivity should be calculated for every single product. But, then, it is difficult to handle properly the difference of quality between different goods. Moreover, the quality difference may very well be larger between different nations than it is within a single country. In addition, there is a difference in quality of labor from one production process to another.

Finally, we have no method of adjusting the difference in relative prices which normally exists between two countries, because of the restriction of data. For some selected goods, of course, the adjustment is possible. But the number of such goods is relatively small.

For these reasons we will calculate value productivity instead of physical. The figures shown in Table III are index numbers of value productivity in the United States and Japan. (They were originally calculated by Shunsaku Nishikawa, associate professor of Keio University, from the 1954 data.) For the computation of the index numbers, Irving Fisher's ideal formula was used, because Nishikawa's data were based on the most detailed classification of industry, whereas our wage statistics are not.

For weighting, the added value of each industry was used instead of the number of laborers. The reason for doing so is that there is no commodity which is produced by labor alone: if we use the added value as a weight, the productivity of other factors of production—capital, land, etc.—is evaluated implicitly; if we use the number of laborers as a weight, on the other hand, the efficiency of other factors is not expressed even on an implicit basis. Suppose that we are aggregating labor productivities of several operations in order to get a productivity figure for an industry as a whole. If we use the number of laborers as a weight, the significance of the industry which employs a large number of laborers shows relatively low labor productivity—e.g., the lumber industry or the fiber industry—tends to be exaggerated, and another industry with a more capitalistic method of production—e.g., the chemical industry—tends to be underestimated. Apparently it does not seem to be appropriate to get such a result.

Moreover, it would be safe to say that the ultimate object of all economic policy is to increase the real national income. Suppose again that a capital-saving industry expands. Unemployment will decrease, but labor productivity in such an industry being relatively low, real wages, and consequently the standard of living in the society, will not improve very much. For this reason, from the policy point of view, the use of the value added as a weight is more desirable.

These are, then, the reasons why we do not use the labor weight for the international comparison of wage rates.

VI. Wages and Productivity

In this section, we will compare labor productivity between the United States and Japan. However, a few words of caution are in order before we discuss the results.

First of all, it is most desirable to obtain "pure" productivity of labor, which is free from changes in environmental factors such as ages, sex, occupation, skills, etc., of workers, and the economic structure. For example, if we use the macro-economic data directly, and divide the sum of products by the number of laborers—this is the conventional method frequently used for computing index numbers of labor productivity—the result (so-called "labor productivity") will include the effects of changes in industrial structure, which are not related to the efficiency of labor itself. To exclude such a possibility, we should start with the micro-economic analysis, and then aggregate each productivity by the method which is analogous to the one used in computation of the index numbers of production. But it is difficult to single out these environmental factors, and, in reality, we are forced to compromise to the conventional method to some degree. For example, we cannot disintegrate the labor productivity down to the level of each production process.

Secondly, it is difficult in Japan to acquire the statistics on hours of labor in many industries. However, we can calculate the labor productivity per head easily. For this reason, we will

concentrate our analysis on the relation between the monthly
wages and the per capita labor productivity.

We have obtained the following results:

(1) When we observe the relationship between wages and
productivity, we note that the difference in wages between the
United States and Japan is always larger than that in labor
productivity. Although the former (wage relationship) is computed for the year 1959 and the latter (productivity relationship)
for the year 1954, I do not think that the difference of time accounts for this observed fact. During the years 1954–59, the
growth rate of labor productivity in Japan was approximately
forty-three per cent, and in America it was twenty-two per cent.
This means that the productivity difference would be reduced
substantially, if we compared the 1959 figures instead of the 1954
ones. Therefore, the mere difference of timing fails to explain
the larger discrepancy in wages than that in productivity. We
should seek another reason to explain this fact.

The following two explanations are suggested as possible reasons for the fact noted above: namely, first, the problems involved
in production function; second, the wage inflation.

Theoretically, wages should be compared with the marginal
productivity of labor. If there is any difference between these
two, it is mainly because of the imperfect competition in the
product market, and/or immobility of labor, and/or inflexibility
of the supply of labor. If we apply the Cobb-Douglas function
to the industry in consideration, the parameter k, the power of
labor, plays an important role. If k for the industry takes the
same value in the United States as it is in Japan, the marginal
productivity ratio for an industry (marginal productivity for
the industry in the United States divided by that in Japan, for
example) may be substituted by the average productivity ratio
(defined likewise).

However, there is no warrant that k takes the same value for
different countries. If the marginal productivity of labor coincides with the wage rates, the value of k in the United States
must actually be larger than that of Japan. This is quite reason-

able, for the relative share of labor in a more developed country is likely to be larger than that of an under-developed country. We may also observe that under perfect competition, or where the degree of monopoly is constant, k is equal to the relative share, provided $k+j=1$ (where j is the power of capital).

Other factors to be considered are wage inflation and the inflexibility of labor supply. The latter disturb the relationship between k and the value of relative share. In addition, the supply is likely to decrease as wages increase.

Let us observe graphically the relationship between wage ratios (wage rates in the United States divided by those in Japan) and productivity ratios. (See Chart 1.) It seems that the changes in wage ratios and productivity ratios affect each other as if they were random shocks. Put differently, the lack of a straightforward relationship may be explained as a short-term phenomenon, for a firm will find little time in the short run, for example, to adjust the resource allocation to the new wage system.

In addition to all this, we should not forget that there is a formidable problem in the computation of the index numbers of wages and productivity.

(2) We can classify the data of manufacturing industries as follows:

> (I) industries where the differences of both productivity and wages are high:
>> (industry code number, 16) fabricated metal products
>> (22) precision machinery
>> (17) machinery
>> (5) furniture;
> (II) industries where the differences of both productivity and wages are low:
>> (2) cotton
>> (7) printing and publishing
>> (20) leather;
> (III) industries where the difference of productivity is high and that of wages is low:
>> non-existent;

(IV) industries where the difference of productivity is com-
      paratively low and that of wages is high:
      (10) rubber products
      (11) food and kindred
      (4)   lumber and wood products.

Chart 1.

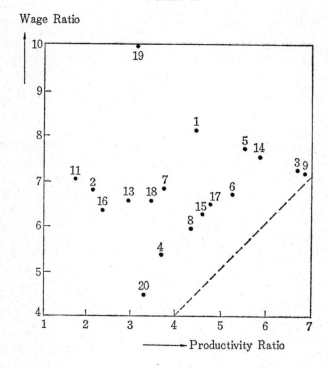

In groups (I) and (II), there are positive correlations between
productivity and wages. Group (I) consists of heavy industries
except for the furniture industry. Group (II) consists of labor-
intensive industries, where labor productivity is likely to be low.
In fact, during 1954–59 the difference of productivity in group
(I) was reduced, and we need to discount the positive correlation
by the amount of the decrease. In the industries included in
(III) and (IV), the positive correlation between productivity and

wages is evidently disturbed. There is nothing common in the production methods, except that non-durable goods bear a common characteristic; it would therefore be natural to consider that it is the condition of product and labor markets that has brought forth the disturbance.

In observing the relationship between wages and productivity ratios, we get the regression line (3.1) $W = \alpha_0 + \alpha_1 P$ where W is the wage ratio, P the average productivity ratio, and α's are parameters. Let us assume that the value of α_1 takes the value which is in the neighbourhood of 1. If the ratio of k's—the power of labor—between two countries is not very different from industry to industry, and if there is a tendency that wage rates approach the value of marginal productivity of labor, α_1 will indeed become very close to 1. This assumption is not so un-realistic as it may seem at first, because the question that we are concerned with is the *ratio* of k's, not the absolute value. Of course, even if we deal with ratios, there is no guarantee that they take the same value in every industry; and, furthermore, the value of α_1 is, in reality, slightly different from 1. In addition, in some industries, there may be a situation where $k + j \neq 1$, and thus k is slightly different from the relative share. Even in such a situation, however, our reasoning is valid, as long as the value of $k + j$ of an industry is close in both countries.

The existence of α_0 is explained by the condition of the labor market. In the United States, owing to the short supply of labor, the possibility of wage inflation is stronger than it is in Japan. Cost inflation has even helped to prevent the business reces-sion, enabling the rate of growth of real wages to exceed that of labor productivity. In Japan, there has been serious unem-ployment; consequently, management has a great deal of power in determining wage rates. The rate of growth of real wages, therefore, has had a tendency to fall short of that of labor pro-ductivity. Recently, the labor supply in Japan has also fallen behind the demand, and the condition of the labor market re-sembles that of the Western countries more and more. Our data do not show this change, since they relate to the period of

1954–59. At any event, these are the reasons why we have added
the constant term α_0 to our regression line, (3.1).

VII. Employment and Productivity

Next, we will analyze the relation between employment and
productivity. In a society where there is severe unemployment,
it may happen that the shift of the marginal productivity curve
of labor, which is caused either by an innovation or by capital
accumulation, does increase employment, provided that the competition among laborers prevents the rate of growth of real wages
from moving upwards as fast as the shift of the marginal productivity curve. In such a case we may observe a positive correlation between the rate of growth of average productivity and
the rate of increase of employment. But there could very well be
a negative correlation also. If an industry adopts a production
method which is excessively labor-intensive in the light of the
optimal factor allocation, it will result in the decrease of labor
productivity by the virtue of the law of diminishing returns to
scale. As more laborers are employed, labor productivity becomes smaller, and we may indeed find a negative correlation
between employment and productivity. These two effects explained above may cancel each other.

We have obtained the following results from our observation
of the data:

(1) In the textile industry, both labor productivity and employment are very high. This positive correlation is so strong
that one may expect to get a positive correlation for the whole
group of industries because of the textile industry.

(2) In the precision-machinery industry, the productivity is
very high, yet the employment is very low. Therefore, we may
infer the existence of a negative correlation for the industry.
But, as mentioned above, we need to take account of the decrease
of the difference in productivity in heavy industries during the
five years in consideration, and if we make adjustment of this
change, the degree of the negative correlation will be decreased

considerably.

Consequently, after all the adjustments in the productivity difference have been made, it is found that the furniture industry is the one that most likely disturbs the existence of the positive correlation. In this industry, the labor productivity is fairly high, but the volume of employment is not correspondingly large.

We will classify the industries, according to the above observation, roughly as follows:

(a) the group where both productivity and employment are high:
- (3) textile
- (4) lumber and wood products
- (9) petroleum and coal products
- (16) fabricated metal products
- (17) machinery;

(b) industries where both productivity and the volume of employment are low:
- (12) glass
- (2) fiber
- (10) rubber products
- (11) leather and leather products
- (14) primary metal.

It should be noted that group (a) consists of finished-goods industries, whereas group (b) are raw-material industries. This symptom may be due, not to the types of production, but to the market conditions. For example, the fact that the textile industry and fiber industry are included in different groups cannot be explained by a mere technical difference between these industries. It may well be ascribed to the difference in market conditions.

In the United States, the price of consumer goods is relatively high and conversely with the price of producers' goods. In Japan the situation is completely opposite. Why does this difference exist?

It seems to me that the reason for this difference is found, first of all, in the existence of relatively high effective demand which raises the value of finished goods, and ultimately increases

the demand for labor. To put this mathematically, let us denote
employment by L and parameters by β, and let (3.2) $L=\beta_0+\beta_1 P$,
where $\beta_1 > 0$, be the demand function of labor. Empirically, β_0 may
take a small value.

What is the meaning of the value of β_0? To answer this question,
we will transform the equation (3.2) and get (3.3) $\beta_1 \cdot \dfrac{P}{L} = 1 - \dfrac{\beta_0}{L}$.
Apparently, the larger is the value of β_0, the smaller becomes the
labor productivity P, and the larger becomes employment. Then the
smallness of the value of β_0 corresponds to the fact that the effect
of diminishing marginal productivity is insignificant. On the other
hand, when the value of β_1 is large, the effect of the diminishing
marginal productivity is strong. Empirically speaking, β_1 does not
seem to show a significant deviation from $\beta_1 = 1$. (See Chart 2)

Next, how should we interpret the variance of the residuals in
(3.2)?

The key to the answer of this question is given by the concept
of "elasticity of demand for labor," suggested by Professor A.C.
Pigou in his book, *Theory of Unemployment*. If we assume that
the Cobb-Douglas production function applies both to the United
States and to Japan, and, in addition to this, that the value of k
in each of the corresponding industries in the two countries is the
same, the following reasoning may follow. Denoting the sum of
products in the United States by Q, and the number of employees
by L; and also denoting the sum of products in Japan by Q', the
number of employees by L', we derive the formula (3.4) below
from the equation (3.2):

$$(3.4) \quad \frac{L}{L'} \cdot \frac{\partial Q'}{\partial L'} = \beta_0 \cdot \frac{\partial Q'}{\partial L'} + \beta_1 \cdot \frac{\partial Q}{\partial L}.$$

Let us find $\dfrac{\partial^2 Q}{\partial L^2}$ from (3.4), assuming that $\dfrac{dL'}{dL} = 0$, which is justified in the short-term analysis where the increase of employment in
the United States affects the employment in Japan; we then have

$$\beta_1 \cdot \frac{\partial^2 Q}{\partial L^2} = \frac{1}{L'} \cdot \frac{\partial Q'}{\partial L'},$$

or, the elasticity of marginal labor productivity η may be obtained as

Chart 2.

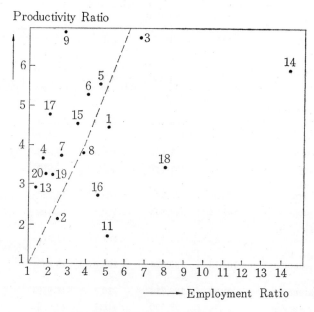

$$(3.5) \quad \eta = \frac{\partial^2 Q}{\partial L^2} \Big/ \frac{\partial Q}{\partial L} = \frac{1}{L - \beta_0 L'} .$$

The elasticity of demand for labor with respect to the change in marginal productivity of labor, E, is given by

$$(3.6) \quad E = \varDelta L \left(1 - \beta_0 \cdot \frac{L'}{L} \right).$$

It is apparent that if the values of β_0 and L' are large, the value of E will be small. Perhaps, β_0 and $\frac{L'}{L}$ take different values in different industries, and so does E. This seems to explain the residual of the regression line (3.2). Since we have not computed the production functien as yet, however, it is necessary to prove our reasoning by the direct computation of this regression formula.

Table I (i). International Comparison of the Wages between the U.S.A.
and Japan in the Manufacturing Industry
(1959)

Industry	(A) U.S. weekly wages (in $)	(B) U.S. weekly wages (in ¥)	(C) U.S. employ-ment (thousand)	(D) Japan monthly wages (in ¥)	(E) Japan employ-ment (thousand)
1 Lumber and wood products	82.01	105,441	628.4	13,043	119
2 Stone and clay	92.06	118,363	467.7	17,462	185
3 Furniture	75.58	97,174	323.9	13,528	48
4 Primary metal	106.67	137,147	609.2	24,916	339
5 Fablicated metal products	99.91	128,883	840.7	16,728	182
6 Machinery	101.02	129,883	1,169.5	19,511	295
7 Electric machinery	90.54	116,409	891.8	17,071	328
8 Transport equipment	108.13	139,024	1,203.9	23,365	313
9 Precision machinery	93.89	120,716	230.2	16,859	86
10 Miscellaneous	76.54	98,936	416.0	12,080	124
11 Food and kindred products	86.53	111,253	1,167.9	15,847	225
12 Tobacco products	63.65	81,836	98.0	20,839	19
13 Fiber	57.45	73,864	890.2	11,226	630
14 Textile mill products	55.85	71,807	1,105.7	9,585	76
15 Pulp and paper	96.54	124,123	458.4	20,001	127
16 Publishing and printing	105.65	135,836	567.6	21,385	122
17 Chemical products	105.33	135,424	540.4	20,970	263
18 Petroleum and coal products	120.18	154,517	153.5	23,532	19
19 Rubber products	102.01	131,156	213.0	13,102	96
20 Leather and leather products	59.25	76,179	335.9	16,994	17

Table I (ii). Wage Ratios and Employment Ratios

Industry	(F) Wage Ratio $\left(\dfrac{B}{D}\right)$	(G) Employment Ratio $\left(\dfrac{C}{E}\right)$
1 Lumber and wood products	8.082	5.27
2 Stone and clay	6.778	2.53
3 Furniture	7.183	6.76
4 Primary metal	5.384	1.80
5 Fabricated metal products	7.679	4.60
6 Machinery	6.658	3.96
7 Electric machinery	6.813	2.72
8 Transport equipment	5.950	3.86
9 Precision machinery	7.160	2.67
10 Miscellaneous	7.991	3.32
11 Food and kindred products	7.020	5.20
12 Tobacco products	3.927	5.15
13 Fiber	6.580	1.41
14 Textile mill products	7.492	14.55
15 Pulp and paper	6.528	3.61
16 Publishing and printing	6.352	4.65
17 Chemical products	6.458	2.06
18 Petroleum and coal products	6.566	8.10
19 Rubber products	10.010	2.22
20 Leather and leather products	4.483	1.96

Table II. F. I. E. S. Data in Each Country

Japan (1959)			U.S.A. (1950)			United Kingdom (1953-4)	
Earning	Consumption	Number of families	Earning	Consumption	The Ratio Number of families	Earning	Number of families
¥	¥		$	$	%	Less than	
1,094	17,232	525	628	1,278	6.3	3 pound	747
7,862	12,449	740	1,577	1,768	12.3	3-6	1,279
12,656	14,324	1,648	2,659	2,718	18.7	6-8	1,437
17,537	17,021	3,281	3,701	3,570	24.0	8-10	2,031
22,317	20,611	4,458	4,796	4,450	16.9	10-14	3,425
27,385	24,164	4,381	5,926	5,257	9.5	14-20	2,578
32,269	28,209	3,552	7,281	6,043	6.4	over 20	1,414
37,284	31,444	2,712	9,350	7,108	3.5		
42,192	34,062	1,985	18,801	10,773	2.4		
47,276	36,985	1,352					
54,315	41,398	1,628					
64,480	45,734	958					
74,501	51,264	544					
83,776	54,904	313					
94,147	57,531	171					
141,761	71,409	403					

The earnings in each country show the incomes before taxation.

Table III. The Index Number of Labor Productivity in the Manufacturing
Industry in U.S.A., 1954

(Japan=100)

1	Food and kindred	169.0
2	Cotton and fibers	291.7
3	Textile	582.8
4	Lumber	440.8
5	Furniture	671.9
6	Pulp	456.1
7	Newspaper	271.9
8	Organic chemical	471.9
9	Petroleum	339.5
10	Tire and tube	323.6
11	Leather	324.3
12	Glass	318.2
13	Cement	166.8
14	Iron	350.2
15	Metal	382.0
16	Metal for construction	549.4
17	Machinery	523.3
18	Electric machine	373.0
19	Machine for correspondence	431.8
20	Ship building	206.8
21	Vehicles	599.8
22	Watch	686.5
23	Manufacturing industry (total)	405.4

Table IV.   The Index Numbers for 1959 (1954=100)
in the Manufacturing Industry

		Japan	U.S.A.
(A)	Employment	140.0	101.0
(B)	Production	200.05	123.0
(C)	Productivity ($=(B)/(A)$)	143.0	122.4
(D)	Nominal Wage	128.0	124.3

Source:

As for Japan, the figures were calculated by the Japanese Economic Planning Agency.

As for the U.S.A., the figures were taken from *Statistics for Foreign Economy* by the Bank of Japan.

CHAPTER 4.

AN INDEX NUMBER OF LABOR PRODUCTIVITY[1]

I. The Problem Defined

Labor productivity increase is one of the most important topics in which economists, businessmen, statisticians and trade unionists are interested. Their interest stems from the fact that a rise in productivity contributes to the rise in standard of living through the distribution of increased income. A number of works, both analytical and empirical, have appeared on this subject. Nevertheless, the definition and meaning of an index of productivity is, even today, not unambiguous.

Normally, indices of employment, production and productivity are defined as follows:

$$(4.1) \quad L_{01} = \sum l_1 / \sum l_0 \text{ (index of employment)}$$

$$Q_{01}^L = \sum p_0 q_1 / \sum p_0 q_0 \text{ (index of production)};$$

$$A_{01}^L = Q_{01}^L / L_{01} = (\sum p_0 q_1 / \sum p_0 q_0) / (\sum l_1 / \sum l_0)$$

$$\text{(index of productivity).}$$

In the formulation, l stands for the number of workers employed in an industry, and p and q indicate commodity price and volume of production respectively. Subscripts 0 and 1 denote base year and comparative year, and the superscript L denotes Laspeyres formula. Of course it is possible to work with the Paasche or Fisher formula, but there is no need to worry about such complications for

---

1) The author is indebted to Professor Lawrence R. Klein of the University of Pennsylvania, who read the earlier draft of this paper and provided helpful suggestions.

the present purpose. $\sum$ means the summation over industries. We may rewrite equation (4.1) as:

$$(4.2) \quad A_{01}^L = \left(\frac{\sum p_0 q_1}{\sum l_1} \right) \bigg/ \frac{\sum p_0 q_0}{\sum l_0} .$$

The numerator on the right-hand side expresses product per worker in the comparative year, evaluated at base year prices, while the denominator expresses average product at base year, evaluated in terms of the same prices. Suppose that there occurred a movement of workers from a relatively low productivity industry (e.g., cotton spinning mills), to a relatively high productivity industry (e.g., chemical products). In such a case, the index A_{01}^L will certainly exceed 100, despite the fact that the labor productivities in these two industries have not increased at all. This suggests that the conventional productivity index is inappropriate for the measurement of aggregate changes in individual productivity (in physical or value terms).

II. A Suggested Solution

In this note I will discuss the shortcomings of the ordinary productivity index and then suggest an alternative formula, free from such defects. It is preferable, from the point of view of economic theory, to construct the index in terms of marginal productivity instead of average productivity. Marginal productivity is indispensable to an analysis of the effect of productivity increase upon income distribution. No one, however, has yet made use of the marginal productivity concept in this connection, since its measurement is extremely difficult. So long as we continue to use the average productivity concept, it is impossible to eliminate the effect of changes in objective conditions such as the effect of other factors and structural change. Similar problems have already been discussed, by Professors S. Kuznets and J. R. Hicks, in the context of the problem of measuring the national income. (Cf. References 1, 2 and 3 in the bibliography).

Let us assume that the Cobb-Douglas production function is suitable for a description of the input-output relationship in every industry.

$$(4.3) \qquad q=bl^k c^j \quad \text{and} \quad k+j=1$$

where c stands for capital stock, and the b, k and j are parameters characterizing the production structure of each industry.

In the case of a Cobb-Douglas type specification, the marginal productivity of labor (4.4a) can be evaluated as the average productivity of labor (4.4b) times the factor (labor) elasticity of product, although a direct assessment of marginal productivity would probably be a troublesome task.

$$(4.4a) \qquad \partial q/\partial l = b(c/l)^j k$$
$$(4.4b) \qquad q/l = b(c/l)^j$$

Comparing (4.4a) and (4.4b), we have:

$$(4.4) \qquad \partial q/\partial l = k(q/l)$$

Our marginal productivity index may then be defined as:

$$(4.5) \quad B_{01}^L = \left(\sum p_0 \frac{\partial q_1}{\partial l_1} \, l_0 \right) \Big/ \left(\sum p_0 \frac{\partial q_0}{\partial l_0} \, l_0 \right)$$

where the value of l_0, i.e. employment in the base year, is used as weights, and the marginal productivities of the base and comparative years are valued in the prices of the base year (p_0). The introduction of p_0 will bring some difficulties to the fore, but these will be discussed later.

Substituting $(\partial q/\partial l)$ from equation (4.4) into equation (4.5), we obtain:

$$(4.6) \quad B_{01}^L = \left(\sum p_0 k \frac{q_1}{l_1} l_0 \right) \Big/ \left(\sum p_0 k \frac{q_0}{l_0} l_0 \right)$$
$$= \left[\sum k p_0 q_0 \left(\frac{q_1}{l_1} \Big/ \frac{q_0}{l_0} \right) \right] \Big/ (\sum k p_0 q_0)$$

The first expression is the so-called "total method" and the second the "relative method" of index calculation. If we compare these two expressions, we find that a *marginal* productivity index calculated by the *total* method using *employment* as weights, completely coincides with an *average* productivity index calculated by the *relative* method using *relative shares* as weights.

Under the assumption of constant returns it is well known that the relative share of labor becomes kpq. When the returns to scale are not constant, but either increasing or decreasing, some errors suggested by Professor P.B. Simpson (*Cf.* Reference 5 in the bibliography) will result. Moreover, under the assumption of perfectly competitive product markets, the above introduction of p_0 into the index formula presents a serious problem. Under the conditions of an imperfect product market, our procedure is never justified, since p cannot be treated as a given "datum" for individual producers. Let e denote the price elasticity of demand for product. We should then have:

$$(4.7) \qquad \frac{p_0}{p_1} \cdot \frac{\partial(p_1 q_1)}{\partial l_1} = \frac{p_0}{p_1}\left(1 - \frac{1}{e}\right) p_1 \frac{\partial q_1}{\partial l_1} = p_0 \left(1 - \frac{1}{e}\right)\frac{\partial q_1}{\partial l_1}$$

from which we get:

$$(4.8) \qquad B_{01}^{L} = \left[\sum k \frac{q_1}{l_1} p_0 \left(1 - \frac{1}{e} l_0\right)\right] \Big/ \left(\sum k \frac{q_0}{l_0} p_0 l_0\right)$$

$$= \left[\sum k p_0 q_0 \left(1 - \frac{1}{e}\right)\left(\frac{q_1}{l_1} \Big/ \frac{q_0}{l_0}\right)\right] \Big/ \sum k p_0 q_0$$

In turn, (4.8) is clearly reduced to (4.6) under perfect market conditions. Professors Court and Lewis have discussed the significance of a production cost index in its relation to physical productivity. In such a situation the adjustment described above will be unnecessary (*cf.* Reference 4 in the bibliography). Professor Kendrick developed an overall productivity index including two or more inputs (*cf.* Reference 6 in the bibliography). The discussion so far has been concerned with one input, i.e. labor; however, we may possibly derive such an overall marginal productivity index following the same procedure, provided that either the estimates of factor elasticities or of factor shares are in our hands.

III. Concluding Remarks

Thus far, we have obtained the result that *an average productivity index weighted by labor share is the same as a marginal productivity index weighted by labor input,* provided that the assumed Cobb-Douglas production function holds good. The index suggested, by equation (4.6), may perhaps be useful for *any* analysis of changes in productivity—or relative share relationships.

It will be useful to illustrate with a numerical example for Japanese manufacturing. During the five years between 1930 and 1935, the indices of production and of employment rose to 167.1 and 132.0. The ordinary labor productivity index A_{01}^L was accordingly equal to 126.5, while the proposed one B_{01}^L was computed as 104.2. To put it in another way, unless B_{01}^L should have been adopted for A_{01}^L, we obtained an upward-biased estimate of productivity increase during the period.

Along the same lines of thought, we can derive some suggestive results concerning the formulation of a real wage index. In its usual form, the index of real wages is defined as:

$$(4.9) \qquad (W/P)_{01}^L = \left(\sum p_0 \frac{w_1}{p_1} l_0\right) \Big/ \left(\sum p_0 \frac{w_0}{p_0} l_0\right)$$

where w indicates nominal wage.

On the other hand, we know that:

$$(4.10) \qquad (w_0/p_0)=(\partial q_0/\partial l_0) \quad \text{and} \quad (w_1/p_1)=(\partial q_1/\partial l_1)$$

Let us define $(W/P)_{01}^L$ as:

$$(4.11) \qquad (W/P)_{01}^L = \left[\sum\left(\frac{w_1}{p_1} \Big/ \frac{w_0}{p_0}\right) w_0 l_0\right] \Big/ (\sum w_0 l_0),$$

where $w_0 l_0$ is the wage bill in the base year.

Inserting equation (4.10) into equation (4.11), we have:

$$(4.12) \qquad (W/P)_{01}^L = \left[\sum\left(\frac{w_1}{p_1} \Big/ \frac{w_0}{p_0}\right) k p_0 q_0\right] \Big/ (\sum k p_0 q_0)$$

If there is no correlation between w and p, equation (4.12) leads to:

$$(4.13) \quad (W/P)_{01}^L = \frac{\left\{\left[\sum \frac{w_1}{w_0}(k p_0 q_0)\right] \Big/ (\sum k p_0 q_0)\right\}}{\left\{\left[\sum \frac{p_1}{p_0}(k p_0 q_0)\right] \Big/ (\sum k p_0 q_0)\right\}} = W_{01}^L/P_{01}^L.$$

In the last expression, W_{01}^L and P_{01}^L mean the nominal wage index and price index (retail or wholesale) respectively. However, neither of them is the usual index of wages and prices, since the weighting systems are labor shares, kpq. It is possible to conclude that a conventional ratio of wage index to price index does not correctly reflect changes in real wages by comparing equations (4.12) and (4.13).

BIBLIOGRAPHY

1. J.R. HICKS, "The Valuation of Social Income", *Economica*, 1940, pp. 105–124.
2. S. KUZNETS, "On the Valuation of Social Income—Reflections on the Professor Hicks' Article," *ibid.*, 1948, pp. 1–17.
3. J.R. HICKS, "The Valuation of Social Income on Professor Kuznets' Reflections," *ibid.*, 1948, pp. 163–172.
4. L.M. COURT and H.G. LEWIS, "Production Cost Indices," *Review of Economic Studies*, 1942–43, pp. 28–42.
5. P.B. SIMPSON, "Transformation Functions in the Theory of Production Index," *Journal of American Statistical Association*, 1951, pp. 225–233.
6. J.W. KENDRICK, "Productivity Trends; Capital and Labor," *Review of Economics and Statistics*, 1956, pp. 248–257.

CHAPTER 5.

LABOR PRODUCTIVITY, INCOME DISTRIBUTION AND SOCIAL CONSUMPUTION FUNCTION

The purpose of this essay is to clarify the effect of increase of labor productivity upon the distribution of income, and aggregate social consumption. We started from the following assumptions. (1) The increase of labor productivity is achieved by means of "innovation" accomplished by large firms, and if this planning has succeeded, small firms will adopt the same productive process. (2) The competition between large and small firms in labor market is incomplete in some degree, and the wages paid by large firms are higher than small firms. (3) Production function takes Cobb-Douglas type. (4) The capitalists are relatively richer class, and wage-earners are poor class. Then we denote by following symbols.

L = laborers employed by large firms.

l = laborers employed by small firms.

Q = output of large firms.

q = output of small firms.

A = average labor productivity in large firms ($=Q/L$).

a = average lobor productivity in small firms ($=q/l$).

K = physical capital employed by large firms.

K' = physical capital employed by small firms.

λ = the inequality in average labor productivity ($=\sum(A-a)$).

According to the assumption (3), $Q=bL^kK^j$, $q=b'l^{k'}K'^{j'}$ (b, k, $j=$ const.) Now, suppose a large firm has succeeded in an innovation process, its labor productivity increased and employed new laborers. Owing to the decrease of production cost, the large firms as well as other small firms will increase the production of that

commodity, and employment. How will be the effect of this result
upon λ? Differenciating λ with L, we get the following equation.

(5.1) $$\frac{\partial \lambda}{\partial L}=\sum\left[\frac{A}{L}(k-1)-\frac{a}{l}\frac{\partial l}{\partial L}(k'-1)\right]$$

The condition that the left side of this equation is negative, is

(5.2) $$\frac{\partial l}{\partial L}\cdot\frac{L}{l}<\frac{1-k}{1-k'}\cdot\frac{A}{a}$$

Probably, the increasing rate of employment by small firms will
be smaller than that of large firms, hence the value of left side
of inequality (5.2) will be smaller than (5.1). The condition that
the value or right side of inequality (5.2) is to be larger than (5.1)
is

(5.3) $$A-a>\frac{\partial Q}{\partial L}-\frac{\partial q}{\partial l}$$

Even if the competition is incomplete, there will be a tendency
to equalize the marginal labor productivity between firms, but
there is no reason to believe that there exists any tendency to
equalize the average labor productivity between firms. So that
inequality (5.3) will be satisfied. When k and k' are constant, and
real wages are determined to be proportionate to marginal labor
productivity, the inequality in real wages will be decreased also.

   How will the capital productivity change?   (1) In case the
production level is constant, the elasticity of substitution between labor and capital will be defined as follows.

(5.4) $$\eta=-\frac{\partial K}{\partial L}\cdot\frac{L}{K}=\frac{k}{j}$$

Then we define average capital productivity as follows.

$$g=Q/K,\ g'=q/K'\ \ \lambda'=\sum(g-g')$$

To observe the effects of increase of labor upon capital, we dif-
ferenciate λ' with L.   Then we get,

(5.5) $$\frac{\partial \lambda'}{\partial L}=\sum\left[\frac{g}{K}(j-1)-\frac{g'}{K'}\cdot\frac{dK'}{dK}(j'-1)\right]\frac{dK}{dL}$$

Substituting (5.4) to (5.5), and examinating $\frac{\partial \lambda'}{\partial K}$ in similar way we
get the result that λ' will be increased by increase of employment.
If the income of capitalist is determined in proportion to marginal

capital productivity, the inequality between incomes of capitalists
will increase.

According to the assumption (5.4), the upper part of higher income class, and lower part of small income class will become to
receive more relative shares. Then, how will the inequality of
distribution of social income change? Starting from Pareto's law
of distribution, we assume that before the achievement of innovation, the Pareto's curve is linear. After the re-distribution by innovation the Pareto's curve will become a curve which is concave
to original point. When we calculate the Pareto's coefficient by
least square method, the value will be larger than theoretical value
of inequality.

Next, we analyse the second case that the production level is
variable. The marginal substitutional rate of labor to capital is

$$(5.6) \qquad \frac{dK}{dL} = \frac{1}{j}\left[\frac{K}{Q}\left(\frac{dQ}{dL} = \frac{\partial Q}{\partial L}\right)\right]$$

$\frac{dQ}{dL}$ is net marginal productivity of labor defined by Professor

Marshall. Perhaps $\frac{dQ}{dL} > \frac{\partial Q}{\partial L}$ and $\frac{dK}{dL} > 0$. Substituting (5.6) to

(5.5), we get the result that $\frac{d\lambda'}{dL} < 0$. By analogical inference to the

former case, the degree of inequality of capital income will decrease, but the degree of decrease will be smaller than that of
labor income. The rate of increase of lower part income of capitalist classes will be smaller than that of relative high wage-
earners. The Pareto's coefficient of inequality is larger than
theoretical value of inequality, but the degree of overestimation
will be smaller than the former case.

Thirdly we consider the Gini's coefficient of inequality. Using
Japanese data, we get the result that the value of Gini's coefficient δ

is smaller than approximate value calculated with $\delta' = \frac{\alpha}{\alpha-1}$ using

Pareto's coefficient α. (See table I) How to explain about this
gap? The condition that Gini curve is complete straight line
before and after innovation is that the rate of income increase is

simultaneously equal for each member. But in our case this assumption is not valid. Let us denote N as the number of income groups, x as the average income of each group, and S as the total income of each group. When we use statistical data, x is calculated as geometrical mean between upper limit value and lower limit value of each income group. If at initial condition Gini curve is complete straight line, for relatively small income groups the increasing rate of S will be larger than that of Nx, and for relatively higher income groups this reasoning is valid too, although the gap between S and Nx is smaller than in the former case. So that,

(5.7) $\log N = \delta \log S - \log C > \delta \log Nx - \log C$

Then, if we calculate from S, the coefficient of Gini's inequality is smaller than theoretical value which is to be calculated from Nx. According to the former reasoning Pareto's coefficient is smaller than theoretical value, and $\delta' = \dfrac{\alpha}{\alpha - 1}$ is larger than theoretical value. Thus we may conclude that δ' is larger than theoretical value, and δ is smaller than it.

When the distribution of income changes in such a manner, how will the social aggregate consumption change? We start from Professor J. Marschak's article, "Personal and Collective Budget Functions" (*Review of Economics and Statistics Vol. XXI*). But his theory assumes that each personal income increases in same proportion. We drop this assumption, and try to explain the change of social expenditure. At initial situation, let us denote r as personal income, $f(r)$ as the number of members receiving the income r, R as the average income of total members, and x as the quantity to consume of each member. X is the average value of x. The m and n are the upper and lower limit of social income groups respectively. Then, r changes to l and R changes to R'.

(5.8) $\displaystyle\int_n^m lf(r)dr = R, \quad X(R) = \int_n^m x\left[l\left(r\dfrac{R'}{R}\right)\right]f(r)dr$

and $\displaystyle\int_n^m \dfrac{\partial l}{\partial R}f(r)dr = 1$.

The social propensity to consume $X'(R)$ is

(5.9) $$X'(R)=\frac{dX}{dR}=\int_{n}^{m}x'(l)\frac{\partial l}{\partial R}f(r)dr$$

This equation shows the correlation between personal and social marginal propensity to consume. Differentiating (9) with R,

(5.10) $$X''(R)=\int_{n}^{m}x''(l)\left(\frac{\partial l}{\partial R}\right)^{2}f(r)dr+\int_{n}^{m}x'(l)\frac{\partial^{2}l}{\partial R^{2}}f(r)dr$$

By this equation we may get the principle of change in social marginal propensity to consume. If personal consumption is linear function of personal income, i.e. $x=a_0+a_1l=a_0+a_1r\dfrac{R'}{R}$ (a is parameter)

(5.11) $$X(R)=\int_{n}^{m}\left(a_0+a_1r\frac{R'}{R}\right)f(r)dr$$

But, in general, "negative consumption" is meaningless. For luxurious goods, when we define $h=-\dfrac{a_0}{a_1}$, we may get

(5.12) $$\begin{aligned}x&=a_0+a_1r \text{ (for the interval } r\geq h)\\x&=0 \ (r<h)\end{aligned}\Bigg\}$$

Further, according to Marschak's theory, we define

$$U(h)=\int_{h}^{m}f(r)dr\div\int_{n}^{m}f(r)dr, \ Z(h)=\int_{h}^{m}rf(r)dr\div\int_{n}^{m}rf(r)dr$$

U and Z are the ratios of members, receiving incomes larger than break-even point, and their total income to total member and income. The Lorenz's coefficient of income inequality λ is

$$\int_{n}^{m}(d-z)\,dz \text{ so that } \frac{d\lambda}{dz}=U(h)-Z(h)$$

Substituting this definition into (8), we get

(5.13) $$X=\sum a_0Z(h)+\sum a_0\frac{d\lambda}{dz}+R\sum a_1z(h)$$

If α_0 and α_1 take same value for each income group, (5.13) can be rewritten as follows,

(5.14) $$X=a_0Z(h)+a_0\frac{d\lambda}{dz}+a_1RZ(h)$$

i.e. the average social consumption depends upon (1) the average social income, (2) the distribution of income, (3) the changing rate of income inequality. According to previous reasoning, technological innovation may have a tendency to equalize the income distribution. Then according to (3), X will be influenced by

$\dfrac{d\lambda}{dz}$. As for liquid assets, we may get similar result by analogical inference.

Next we will examine this reasoning by statistical data. As for pre-War period, 1923–1936, we get

$$(5.15) \qquad C_t = 65.0 + 0.500\,Y_{t-1} \ (r=0.715) \ (\text{unit is yen})$$
$$(7.42) \quad (0.116)$$

Table I				
year	Y	C	Gini's-coefficient	
	yen	yen	δ	δ'
1923	145	132	2,0909	
1924	155.5	129	2,0187	
1925	166.5	130	2,1324	
1926	172.5	148.5	2,1486	2.38
1927	173	158.5	2,2024	2.47
1928	175	156	2,1961	2.50
1929	185	159	2,2068	2.50
1930	191	171	2,2395	2.51
1931	193	167	2,1750	2.43
1932	195	164	2,1766	2.70
1933	195	163	2,1533	2.66
1934	202	164	2,2094	2.55
1935	208	155	2,3390	2.48
1936	212	158	2,1548	2.50
1947	112	95		
1948	127	105		
1949	144	114		
1950	168	121		
1951	183	131		
1952	197	151		
1953	206	162		
1954	209	166		
1955	230	176		
1956	250	183		
1957	262	189		
	(in 1934—1936 price level)			

Table II	
Family Budget Data at Sept. 1926—Aug. 1927	
Monthly income	Food consumption function
yen	yen
50— 70	0.225 Y + 14.6
70— 90	0.225 Y + 14.6
90—110	0.225 Y + 14.6
110—130	0.150 Y + 21.2
130—150	0.150 Y + 21.2
150—170	0.125 Y + 26.5
170—190	0.125 Y + 26.5
190—210	0.100 Y + 31.0
210—230	0.100 Y + 31.0

C is the social real consumption per head and Y shows average real income. The coefficient of correlation is not so large, and we try to introduce Gini's coefficient of inequality δ, (see Table I) then $\gamma_{C\delta}$ is 0.545, and $\gamma_{Y\delta}$ is 0.608. But unfortunately, computing by linear equation, we get

$$(5.16) \qquad C_t = -62.2 + 1.205\,Y_{t-1} - 0.1035\delta$$

The result that the value of coefficient of Y is greater than 1 is not consistent with *a priori* economic information. Perhaps this is the result of multi-correliarity. Further, according to family budget data, the parameter in equation (13) takes different value for each income group. As we neglect this fact and have fitted linear equation, equation (16) has error caused by this procedure. (See Table II)

As for the post-War period, 1947–1957, we get

$$(5.17) \qquad C_t = 28.03 + 0.665\,Y_{t-1} \quad (r = 0.987)$$
$$(4.67) \quad (0.035)$$

As in the post-War period C and Y increased simple-harmonically and very rapidly, the coefficient of correlation is so high, and when we use 1923–36 and 1947–57 statistical data, we get

$$(5.18) \quad C_t = 38.70 + 0.6386\ Y_{t-1} - 3.6082x, \quad (R = 0.940)$$
$$(6.80)\ (0.046) \qquad (2.151)$$

where x is discontinuous variable. ($x = 0$ for pre-War and $x = 1$ for post-War period.) Similarly we computed clothes, etc. Using quarterly National Income data, during 1953–1957, we get;

Food consumption	$C = 3864.2 + 0.18388\,Y$	$(r = 0.9556)$
Fuels and light	$C = 262.45 + 0.008950\,Y$	$(r = 0.950)$
Clothes	$C = 767.8 + 0.44813\,Y$	$(r = 0.5877)$
Housing	$C = 12.90 + 0.0f0435\,Y$	$(r = 0.9224)$

As for Food and Housing, the coefficient of correlation is so high, and consistent with the result calculated from cross-section data, but about clothes and fuels, coefficient of correlation is not high and inconsistent with cross-section data. Perhaps one factor of this is the changes in the distribution of income and another is the peculiar character of durable goods.

Thus, we can get some following conclusions.

(1)   Assuming the Cobb-Douglas production function, if there is
      any unemployment, the improvement of labor productivity
      in large firms by technical innovation will decrease the dif-
      ference of labor productivity and wage between large firms
      and small firms.

(2)   In this case, the Pareto's coefficient of inequality or distribu-
      tion of income will show the large value in comparison with
      theoretical value.   And Gini's coefficient will show the smal-
      ler value than theoretical value.

(3)   By qualifying Professors Marschack's reasoning, the con-
      sumption of each commodity will depend upon the (1) per
      capita income, (2) the distribution of income and (3) per
      capita liquid assets.   In this case the luxurious goods defined
      by Professor Allen and Bowley will decrease relatively and
      the necessaries will increase.   Calculating for Japanese
      data, owing to the multi-correliarity, we can not get the suf-
      ficient results, but the figures in tables will not deny our
      reasoning.   (This paper is abstracted from my book *"A
      Study in the Theory of Wages"*, 1959, written in Japanese.)

CHAPTER 6.

AN INTENATIONAL COMPARISON ABOUT THE CHANGES IN PRICES AND WAGES

I. Introduction

Against the background of an inflationary air in the Japanese economy since around the close of the "Iwato boom", various opinions have been put forth on the question whether the recent rise in prices has been caused by "demand pull" or by "cost push". Outstanding apparent facts are these: With the economic growth employment opportunities have been increased; This has resulted in narrowed wage differentials, particularly in the form of wage rises in medium-small size enterprises and tertiary industries; This has brought about a transformation in the price structure, in which prices for those industries employing labor-intensive pattern of production have been relatively pushed up; On the other side, a rise in the nation's standard of living has caused changes in the structure of effective demands and price rises in some certain commodities. Preferably economists call such a series of facts "a shift of price structure toward the Western pattern." Indeed it may be the case in some sense. Then, we want to question, how is the Western pattern with respect to the wage structure?

According to B. Ohlin's theory, under a condition of liberalized foreign trade price structures of two countries become similar; in the less developed country wages rise and capital costs fall, bringing about a new equilibrium. This argument, however, is one from a view-point of static "long-run". There, the processes of adaptation up to the birth of new equilibrium are put aside from consideration, and also the effects of capital accumulation are not taken into account. So far, an inductive theory grasping these factors from a dynamic viewpoint is not yet completed, and we must concentrate our study on empirical analysis. In a former article* the writer observed the inter-relations between productivity, employment and wages, so to speak the economy of labor, in European countries and America. As many years have passed thereafter, this paper intends a further study for the ten ensuing years**, to present a reference material for outlooking the coming course of the Japanese economy.

In the above said former analysis, covering the period from the immediate postwar time through 1954, we obtained following findings:

(1) Japan, Italy and India are suffering from surplus population, while postwar Britain and France are being worried by shortage of labor force, especially for the necessary export promotion. In America some degree of unemployment, say, frictional unemployment, is remaining. West Germany experienced a period of confusion in early postwar years due to the destruction by war, but the reconstruction in later years has brought her near to the pattern of Britain and France.

(2) Accordingly in Britain and France the employment problem has not come into the open; instead, the wage problem is presenting itself. Wages are determined mainly by the conditions on the part of labor supply.

(3) In Japan, Italy and India the expansion of economic scale is reflected mainly in the rising wage level, rather than in the employment level. This indicates a dissolution of latent unemployment.

(4) A wage policy of Keynesian type may be useful with re-

* "Chinginseisaku to Koyoseisaku" (Wage Policy and Employment Policy), in Toyokeizai Shimposha, ed., Chinginmondai to Chingin Seisaku (Wage Problems and Wage Policy), 1959.
** Up to about 1962, the most recent year data are available at the writing of this paper.

spect to the conditions of demand and supply of labor in the 1930s, but the major concerns of trade unions in those countries where the postwar inflation had been undergone are the real wages.

(5)   In less developed countries common laborers are abundant, while skilled workers are scanty. This is due to the unbalanced developments of industrial techniques and the widencss of qualitative differentials within labor. It is working as a factor impeding the attainment of full employment. Contrarily in America differentials in wages are tending to contract.

(6) The correlationship between labor productivity and real wages is unexpectedly closer in less developed countries than in advanced countries. Such phenomenon, contradicting the existence of unemployed labor, is due to a kind of "uncompetitive group" existing in labor market for the above mentioned reason. A rise in proudctivity is immediately reflected in wages, because, on the ground of low standard of national living, there is no room to utilize such rise in productivity for the sake of social security or the like. And, as for employment problem, the marginal productivity theory appears to be applicable as it is, because the demand function of labor works upon employment with big weight. In contrast, in developed countries the supply function of labor exerts more strength, and so the fruit of a rise in productivity can be directed to enriching social security expenditures and the like. This is, so to speak, the result of the high standard of living.

(7)   In France and Britain the wage fund theory is affecting favorably for labor, while in less developed countries unfavorably. However, the share of labor in income distribution is lower in France, where labor is in shortage, than in Britain and America. Hence, we can see, the factor determining the share lies mainly on the side of demand for labor, and the conditions on the side of supply are only secondary.

(8)   For a stable level of employment, however, the supply of labor must be more inelastic in relation to the demand.

(9)   In France, in spite of the shortage of labor, the prolongation of roundabout production has not been so positively pursued.

This seems to have been one of the reasons why the labor's share
has not grown higher.

(10)   Böhm-Wicksell's new wage fund theory asserts that a
prolonged roundabout production brings about an employment
decline.   Such phenomenon can be seen actually only in India.
In Japan and Italy positive decreasing of employment is not recognized, owing to the parallel advance in capital accumulation.

(11)   Reconstruction plannings of almost all countries are
found to have been under-estimation in the light of performances.
This was caused by the under-estimation on investment propensity and investment efficiency, which had been effected by the low
production activity in the early phase of reconstruction as well
as by the technical innovation thereafter.

(12)   Alone in America business cycles are seen to some extent.
Other countries have been faced with inflation, and a promotion
of saving is required.   Hayek's conclusions in his "Profits, Interest and Investment" are appropriate in less developed countries.

II.   The Situation of U.S.A. since 1953

The above was the conclusions we reached on the economic
situations up to 1954.   Now we must go into the analysis of the
later period.   We shall begin with the data of America, relying
mostly on the statistical figures in the "Kaigai Keizai Tokei"
(Economic Statistics of Foreign Countries) compiled by the Statistical Bureau, Bank of Japan.   In Table I, the first impression
we have is that the growth of national income for the recent eight
years has been very unstable, presenting an appearance of cyclical
movement with periodic time of four years.   It is far from one
deserving a name of steady growth.   Wholesale prices have risen
by about 8 per cent for the ten years 1953–62, but remained stable
for the later five years 1958–62.   Between the rises in wholesale
prices and consumer prices no significant gap is seen.   In 1958–62,
however, consumer prices registered a gradual rise in contrast to
stabilized wholesale prices.   The relative share of earned income
in distribution has been on sustained increase; during the 1940s

it was some 65 per cent, but in 1957 it topped at 70 per cent, being thereafter the same or a little higher. This does not contradict the above stated conclusion (7) in the preceding section.

The national income of America is distributed into industries as follows for 1961;

Agriculture, forestry & fishery	4.3%	Mining	1.2%
Manufacturing	28.4%	Construction	5.2%
Transportation & communication	8.3%	Commerce	16.3%
Administration & defence	13.2%	Others	23.2%

Table I. Relevant Economic Indicators for America

	Industrial Production Index	Employment Index	Hourly Wages (cents)	Wholesale Price Index	Consumer Price Index
1953	100	100	177	100.0	100.0
54	94	93	181	100.2	100.3
55	106	96	188	100.5	100.1
56	109	98	198	103.8	101.6
57	110	98	207	106.8	105.1
58	102	91	213	108.3	108.0
59	116	95	222	108.5	108.9
60	119	96	229	108.6	110.6
61	120	93	232	108.2	111.7
62	129	96	243	108.5	115.7

	Productivity Index	Real Wage Index	Nominal National Income (billion dollars)	Growth of National Income (%)	Share of Earned Income (%)
1953	100	100	305.6		68
54	101	102	301.8	−1.24	69
55	110	105	330.2	9.40	69
56	111	108	350.8	6.25	69
57	112	110	366.9	4.60	70
58	112	111	367.4	0.00	70
59	122	115	400.5	9.20	70
60	124	119	415.5	3.75	71
61	129	121	427.8	2.96	71
62	135	127	453.7	6.05	71

The tertiary industry is carrying a substantial weight, but obviously manufacturing makes the major axis sustaining economic growth. So we shall consider with respect to manufacturing the inter-dependencies between labor productivity, real wages and employment. Here the level of real wages is obtained by deflating nominal wages for "wholesale" prices. It is the ratio between prices of product and wages that primarily concerns the demand function of labor, which in the context of the whole community may be presented as the ratio between wholesale prices and wages.

Chart 1 illustrates their correlation. In the ten years in question labor productivity (dividing index of manufacturing production by index of employment) showed a high rise of 35 per cent. Also real wage index increased broadly in parallel but in slower pace, leaving time lags of one or two years. Employment was on a downward trend. It appears from these facts that, although

Chart 1. Behaviors of Productivity, Real Wages and Employment in America

changes in the industrial structure were somewhat interwoven in the rise in productivity, the rise was mainly achieved through a relation of high wages—need of employment decrease—advance of mechanization. It may have been the case at least in business sense. In effect, a large increase in investment outlays has brought about the results as seen in Chart 1. This is a trend appreciably different from that before 1952.

III. The Industrial Structure of U.S.A.

Now we shall try a theoretical analysis of the effects of a change in labor productivity upon the levels of wage and employment. Let q denote volume of output, p price of product, l number of labor, w nominal wage. Suppose an increase in effective demand has caused an increase in the value of q. Since

$$q = \frac{q}{l} \cdot l, \quad l\frac{d\left(\frac{q}{l}\right)}{dq} + \frac{q}{l}\frac{dl}{dl} = 1.$$

If the elasticity of labor productivity with respect to output is shown by e_q, and similar elasticity of employment by e_l, we can write, similarly with the case of Keynes's elasticity of effective demand, $eq + e_l = 1$. The former term presents the rate of rise in average productivity (and, if the form of production function remains unchanged, the marginal productivity of labor, hence, real wages) to be caused by the effect of demand increase upon q. The latter term shows the rate of contribution to increasing employment.

Let's observe Chart 2. First, we suppose an increase in effective demand has arisen without accompanying technical innovation and capital accumulation. In this case, we may consider only with regard to Curve I, i.e. the curve of marginal productivity of labor. The volume of employment at start is shown by OA, and the marginal productivity by AB. In order to increase q, employment must be enlarged to OC. In the new equilibrium the marginal productivity will be CD. The change in productivity here is expressed with;

$$(6.1) \qquad \frac{d\left(\frac{q}{l}\right)}{dq} = \frac{1}{l}\left(1 - \frac{q}{l}\frac{dl}{dq}\right)$$

Since no shift in the marginal productivity curve is assumed; the second term in parenthesis of the right side is the reverse of k in Douglas production function. In other words, so long as no technical innovation or capital accumulation occures, the changes in q and q/l point toward reverse diretions. When, however, by technical innovation or capital accumulation the marginal productivity curve shifts to position II, the relations will be different. dq/dl in formula (6.1) represents CE in Chart 2, not CD. If O denotes the variable quantities at the base time-point and I denotes those after a shift in the marginal productivity curve, and if the proposition that marginal productivities of labor equal real wages respectively at base time-point and at any given time-point holds good, the height of AB equals w_0/p_0 and that of CE equals w_1/p_1. Then, dq/dl in formula (6.1) becomes $\dfrac{w_1}{p_1} - \dfrac{w_0}{p_0}$, and the whole of formula (6.1) can be rewritten as;

$$(6.2) \qquad \frac{d\left(\dfrac{q}{l}\right)}{dq} = \frac{1}{l_0}\left[1 - \left(\frac{w_1}{p_1} - \frac{w_0}{p_0}\right)\frac{q_0}{l_0}\right]$$

The sign of formula (6.2) depends on the degree of the shift in the marginal productivity curve and that of the increase in em-

Chart 2.

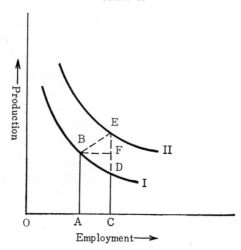

ployment. As the shift in the marginal productivity curve is always arising more or less in dynamic process, simultaneous increases in both productivity and employment due to demand increase are possible. In the case of manufacturing in America 1953–61, however, the substitution effect between labor and capital seems to have been more influential than the increases in productivity and employment. Its reason may lie in the fact that steady rise in national income was not expected and signs of business fluctuation were recognized. While the growth rate of nominal national income for the ten years was 50 per cent, money wage in manufacturing showed an increase of only 37 per cent. Isn't this a result of prolonged roundabout production?

Then, what a structural change is seen in American industry? Table II presents the changes in employment and wages by industrial (median grouping) sections, between September, 1959 and September, 1962. (U.S. Department of Labor, Monthly Labor Review). By the figures we have an impression that the structure of American industry is more unstable than it appears to be. In contrast to the increases in employment for primary metals, arms and rubber goods sections, decreases are seen for sections of miscellaneous manufacturing, oil & gas, machinery and wooden goods. Whether such changes are reflecting the prolongation of roundabout production or not, we cannot say from our data alone (because of, for instance, decreased employment for machinery section). Sections showing high rate rise in nominal wages are textile, machinery, transport equipment and tobacco manufacturing. In contrast the rates are low for wooden goods and rubber sections. We can find no direct correlationship between the level of wages and the rate of wage increase. In textile, machinery, transport equipment and miscellaneous manufacturing the high rates of wage increase are conceived to have been the cause of decrease in employment. For tobacco and fabrics sections the rates of wage increase are relatively high and those of increase in employment are low. Contrarily an industry showing low rate of wage increase and high rate of employment rise is rubber manufacturing. This reverse correlation is

disturbed by primary metals and wooden goods sections. For
these two sections, however, a big change in effective demand

Table II. Changes in Wages and Employment in America,
by industrial sections

	1959 (Sept.)		1962 (Sept.)		Change	
	Wages (A) (dollars)	Employ-ment (B) (1000 persons)	Wages (C) (dollars)	Employ-ment (D) (1000 persons)	(C)/(A) %	(D)/(B) %
0. Arms manufact.	105.22	71.1	116.31	101.1	8.64	42.20
1. Wooden goods	82.01	628.4	82.01	566.2	0	−9.90
2. Stone & glass	92.06	467.7	101.50	480.5	9.15	2.74
3. Furniture & home appliances	75.58	323.9	81.54	322.7	6.96	−0.37
4. Primary metals	106.67	609.2	118.40	911.9	11.00	49.80
5. Metal goods	99.91	840.7	106.91	872.8	7.00	3.60
6. Machinery	101.02	1,169.5	112.74	1,020.7	16.00	−12.75
7. Electrical equipment & appliances	90.54	891.8	99.22	1,060.1	9.60	18.75
8. Transport equipment	108.13	1,203.9	124.49	1,136.2	15.10	−5.62
9. Precision instrument	93.89	230.2	99.72	230.9	6.20	0.03
10. Miscellaneous manufact.	76.95	416.0	78.01	336.0	13.60	−19.25
11. Food	86.53	1,167.9	93.18	1,319.6	7.68	13.00
12. Tobacco	63.65	98.0	71.34	99.9	12.05	1.94
13. Textiles	57.45	890.2	67.54	795.5	17.60	−10.50
14. Clothes	55.85	1,105.7	61.69	1,126.9	10.45	1.91
15. Paper	96.54	459.4	104.49	484.9	8.25	5.56
16. Printing & book binding	105.65	567.6	109.91	603.1	4.02	6.43
17. Chemicals	105.33	540.4	110.81	524.5	5.20	−2.94
18. Oil & coal	120.18	153.5	130.90	125.0	8.94	−18.50
19. Rubber	102.01	213.0	102.42	309.4	0.04	45.20
20. Leather	59.25	335.9	64.53	319.9	8.93	−3.62
21. Mining	107.71	478.0	112.88	514.0	4.80	7.54
22. Wholesale trade	91.53	2,668.0	97.51	2,666.0	6.54	0
23. Retail trade	67.82	8,377.0*	66.70	8,527.0*	1.68	1.79

Note: Wages are weekly wages; employment is production workers,
except retail trade with all workers.

is thinkable. Excepting these, generally the phenomenon of mechanization appears to have emerged being promoted by high
wages.

IV. Correlation between Productivity and Wages in America

Next, how is it about the correlation between productivity and
wages by cross section analysis? In Table III, production indices
by industrial (median group) sections are respectively contrasted
to employment indices computed from Table II. As the grouping
in production indices is relatively crude, in order to adjust for
the difference between two indices we include electrical equipment
and precision instruments into machinery, textiles and fabrics
into clothes & textiles, and rubber into chemicals & oil. For employment index man-days index is employed, and wage index is
the average weighted by 1961's employment. The correlation between indices of productivity rise and wage increase is figured
in Chart 3. The picture as a whole is rather random. Equality
between two indices is recognizable only for (1) metal ware manufacturing, (3) transport equipment and, to a lesser degree, for
(7) paper manufacturing & printing. (As wholesale prices were
stable for this period, the gap between value productivity and
physical productivity seems to have been not so large. For a
more precise analysis an examination by commodity groups may
be necessary.) For primary metals processing, with a big increase in employment, wages increased in spite of decreasing
productivity. A similar trend is seen for food processing to a
certain degree, but in most sections the rate of wage increase
is lower than that of productivity growth. As for commerce (in
Chart 3, No. 11) calculation is based on the following data.

	1958	1961
Commercial income	66.57 bill. dollars	69.63 bill. dollars
Consumer price index	108.00	111.70
Employment	107.50 thousand	113.65 thousand

Note; we take consumer prices because distribution costs are
involved in the income of commerce.)

By the calculation on these data, per-head real income (labor
productivity) for 1961 presents 95.5 per cent of that for 1958; a
decline.   On the other hand, nominal wages rose to 105.0 per cent
in 1959–62; to take the rise in consumer prices, 100.05 per cent.
It is thinkable that this increase in distribution cost gave birth
to the gap, though slight, between consumer and whole-sale prices.
Since the wage level in retail trade was low, being next to textiles
and leather, as seen in Table II, nominal wages must have been
raised even without rise in productivity, if the labor mobility was
large.

Table III.   Correlation between Productivity and Wages
in America, by Industries

	Production Index (1958—61)	Employment Index (1959—62)	Productivity	Nominal Wage Index
1. Primary metals	113	150	75.5	111.0
2. Metal products	114	104	109.5	107.0
3. Transport equipment	106	94	112.5	115.4
4. Machinery	122	101	121.0	111.4
5. Wood	105	90	116.5	100.0
6. Clothes & textiles	117	97	120.5	113.3
7. Paper & printing	116	106	109.5	105.8
8. Chemicals & oil	124	105	118.0	103.9
9. Food & drinks	111	113	98.3	107.7
10. Mining	108	108	100.0	104.8

Supposedly reflecting the advance in mechanization, unemployment increased as follows.

1955......2,900 thousand persons   1959......3,810 thousand persons
1956......2,820   ″   1960......3,930   ″
1957......2,940   ″   1961......4,810   ″
1958......4,680   ″   1962......4,010   ″

Of course, increasing labor population had been making the
background, but such increase in unemployment resulted from
one of two causes; the expansion of economic scale was not large
enough to absorb growing labor population, or, the inducement

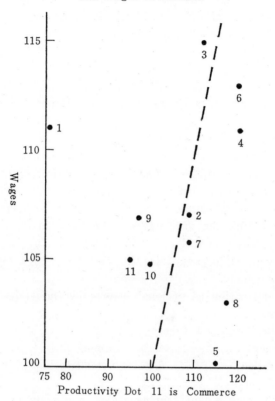

Chart 3. Correlation between Productivity
and Wages in America

of capital was brisk to replace labor. The latter seems to have
been the case by our above analysis. If so, it means that Böhm-
Wicksell's new wage fund theory applies in advanced countries
also.

Lastly, we shall examine data on agriculture.

	1958		1961	
Agricultural Population	5,844	thousand persons	5,463	thousand persons
Index of Production	100	"	125	"
Productivity Index	100.0	"	133.4	"

Due to such rise in productivity agricultural prices dropped
to 92.5 per cent in 1961 (base 1958), in contrast to wholesale
prices remaining stable for the three years. (Agricultural population make up only less than 10 per cent of total labor power.)

V. The Situation of Britain

In Britain, nominal national income has shown a near "steady
growth", the share of earned income in distribution being on a
gradual rise.   This is a small difference from the case in America,
but the growth of nominal national income owes to inflation in
no small measure.   While in America the rise in consumer prices
was 16 per cent for the ten years, it marked as high as 31 per cent
in Britain.   Also wholesale prices there turned to a rising trend
since 1959.   And, the gap between the rises in consumer and
wholesale prices was wider than in America.   In view of these
facts it is impossible to appraise the remarkably high rate growth
of British economy.

The composition of national income by industries for 1956
is as below.

Agriculture, forestry & fishery 4.4%
Manufacturing.................44.1%   Mining 3.7%
Administration.................. 6.4%   Commerce.................12.7%
Finance & services............14.7%

In Britain also manufacturing makes obviously the trunk of
economic development.   Major indicators for manufacturing are
shown in Table IV, and correlations between productivity, level of
real wages and employment are figured in Chart 4.

There is a great difference from the case in America on the
following points.

(1)   The rate of productivity rise for the ten years is 17 per
cent, far lower than 35 percent in America.   This difference in
pace is reflected in the difference of price rise rate.

(2)   Although a small decrease in employment occured in 1958,
the trend of employment has been on gradual increase in contrast to that in America.   Also factors are few that suggest

Table IV.   Relevant Economic Indicators for Britain

	Industrial Production Index (A)	Employment (B) (1000 persons)	Industrial Employment Index (C)	Hourly Wages (D) (pences)	Wholesale Price Index (E)	Consumer Price Index
1953	100	8,746	100	49.2	(100)	100.0
1954	106	8,976	103	52.5	100.0	101.8
1955	116	9,206	105	56.9	103.4	106.4
1956	112	9,269	106	61.1	106.7	111.7
1957	114	9,271	106	65.3	110.2	115.8
1958	113	9,147	104	67.1	111.0	119.3
1959	120	8,477	105	70.0	111.4	120.0
1960	127	8,811	109	76.8	113.1	121.2
1961	128	8,928	110	81.5	115.7	125.3
1962	129	8,852	110	84.5	118.0	130.5

	(A)/(C) (Productivity)	(D)/(E) (Real Wages)	National Income (in million pounds)	Growth of National Income	Share of Earned Income
1953	100		14,910		65%
1954	103	100	15,896	6.6%	65
1955	106	105	16,821	5.8	67
1956	106	109	18,412*	7.7	67
1957	108	113	19,492	5.9	67
1958	109	115	20,281	4.3	67
1959	114	120	21,125	4.2	68
1960	116	129	22,395	6.0	68
1961	116	134	23,694	5.8	69
1962	117	136	24,520	3.5	69

* A year of revision

rapid advance in mechanization. Employment increases by industrial (median group) sections 1958–61 are as follows:

Machinery industry ....0.7%   Total manufacturing...−2.5%
Car & wheel industry ...−25.8%   Construction.................8.4%
Metal industry ....12.5%   Textile industry 3.4%

These figures are somewhat rough since there is a small change in the contents of labor survey between the two years. But we can see an increase in metal industry, in contrast to a decrease

Chart 4. Behaviors of Productivity, Real Wages and Employment in Britain

in machinery industry. As for production index, rises in 1958–61 are:

Total manufacturing av. ...14.7%   Textiles.........................11%
Cement & related goods ...22 %   Food 10%
Steel ....14 %   Wooden goods...............16%
Non-ferrous metals ....16 %   Paper...........................20%
Machinery........................13 %   Construction 20%
Chemicals ....24 %   Mining....................−0.7%

High rate rises for cement and chemicals are noticeable, but we cannot find definite data to conclude a prolongation of roundabout production.

(3) The increase in real wages is far exceeding productivity, which may be a cause for inflation. The rate of unemployment moved:

1956 ....1.2%   1957 ....1.4%
1958 ....2.1%   1959 ....2.2%
1960 ....1.6%   1961 ....1.5%
1962 ....1.9%

Although there are some fluctuations accompanying business cycles, any sign of structural unemployment following the prolongation of roundabout production, as is seen in America, is unrecognizable. It may be said that this is also making the worry of Britain with inflation and low rate of production growth.

Figures of incomes by industrial sectors are available only up to 1960 at the writing. Data on commerce for 1958–60 are:

Growth rate of commercial income 11.40%

Rate of consumer price rise 1.76%

Rate of employment increase.......................................12.00%

The rate of rise in productivity, calculated from these figures, shows 7.7 per cent, surpassing that of manufacturing. This appears to tell the major reason why the gap between wholesale and consumer prices did not widen during the years. In 1961, however, the gap was enlarged, in spite of increasing retail sales and supposable rise in productivity.

The rate of the rise in retail prices for the five years 1956–61 is 14 per cent. High rate is seen for housing, services, light and heat expenses, sundry goods and communication charges, and low rate for consumer durables, alcohol drinks and clothes. This difference by commodity groups resembles the case in Japan, excepting food with 9 per cent, lower than the average. In Britain food depends substantially on import, but as for domestic agriculture we have:

	1956	1961
Production index ...	100	150
Employment	1,032 thousand persons	943 thousand persons

A 65 per cent rise in productivity is seen in the five years. Perhaps this makes one of the factors preventing sharp rise in food price.

On the above descriptions we may conclude:

(1) In Britain we cannot find materials for positive negation of the proposition that rate of productivity change affects relative prices.

(2) For manufacturing, real wages have risen beyond the rise in productivity, and employment has remained unchanged

or showed gradual increase making a cause for inflation. This seems to suggest the inappropriateness of an explanation from the side of demand for labor, that is to say the demand for labor, being promoted by increasing effective demand and production, resulted in the increases in wages and employment. Rather, it seems to tell the predominance of the behaviors of the supply side due to labor shortage. In order to prevent such wage-price spiral, mechanization and productivity rise are necessary. But we can find no index reflecting the prolongation of roundabout production, maybe due to the shortage of capital accumulation.

(3) The share of labor in income distribution has been on gradual rise, but yet lower than in America. This appears to have correlation with the difference in total amount of national income.

VI. France and Italy

In France the growth rate of nominal national income is fairly high, and that showing nearly a steady growth. Its growth rate is higher than that of Britain, although prices rose somewhat higher. Major economic indicators are shown in Table V, and the correlations between productivity, real wages and employment in Chart 5. The rise in productivity for nine years recorded 81 per cent, far exceeding 17 per cent of Britain and 35 per cent of America (both for ten years). This may be an effect of the equipment modernization. Productivity jumped over real wages of 48 per cent increased and employment of 8 per cent increase. It is well inferable that the surplus born from the higher rise in productivity was directed to the capital accumulation for modernization. The share of earned income in distribution is lower than in Britain, but gradually increasing. Perhaps this owes to the fact that, through mechanization, the marginal productivity curve shifted upward. The prolongation of roundabout production is laterally given evidence by production indices of manufacturing by sections, below; for 1961, basic year 1952:

Mining 115   Rubber manufact. 175
Power industry 178   Textiles.............................138
Steel 163   Leather.............................111
Non-ferrous metals 230   Paper................................232
Metal processing 183   Construction 129
Construction materials......162   Chemicals..........................338

Table V. Relevant Economic Indicators for France

	Industrial Production Index	Employment Index	Wages (hourly, francs)	Wholesale Price Index	Consumer Price Index	Productivity	Real Wage Index	National Income	Growth of National Income	Share of Earned Income
1953	100	100	124.2	100	100.0	100	100	1,116		
1954	110	101	131.5	97	99.7	109	109	1,190	6.6%	58%
1955	120	101	141.6	97	101.8	119	117.5	1,292	8.6	58
1956	133	103	152.4	102	102.8	129	120	1,433	10.9	59
1957	145	106	164.4	106	105.5	137	124.5	1,596	11.4	59
1958	151	107	183.8	113	121.4	141	131	1,800	12.8	60
1959	156	105	194.8	120	128.9	148.5	131	1,934	7.5	61
1960	174	106	2.11	125	133.9	164.5	136	2,150	11.1	61
1961	184	107	2.25	129	138.0	172	140	2,332	7.8	62
1962	195	108	2.45	133	144.5	180.5	148			

Chart 5. Behaviors of Productivity, Real Wages and Employment in France

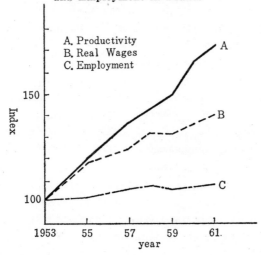

A. Productivity
B. Real Wages
C. Employment

The rates are high for chemicals, paper, non-ferrous metals and metal processing, while low for leather, mining and textiles. This represents the intensification of industrial structure in this country making a great contribution to the rise in productivity.

Also in this country consumer prices have risen faster than wholesale prices, but the gap is observed only after 1958, having no correlation with the growth rate of nominal national income. We cannot analyze the distribution costs to due lack of data, but we can point out marked rises in the prices of labor service from data on consumer price rises by groups for 1956–61; high rises for services (155.0%), amusements (150.5%), housing and rent (181.8%) and communication expenses (144.0%), and low rate rises for home appliances (120.9%), milk & egg (122.7%) shoes & textile goods (122.5%) and vegetables (125.6%). The index of agricultural production showed a 46 per cent rise for three years, making a good help to restrain price rise. The change in price structure in this country resembles that of our country, but the rise in agricultural prices is moderate, in common with Britain.

Major indicators for Italy are provided in Table VI. The growth rate of nominal national income is a little higher than in Britain and lower than in France and W. Germany. Wholesale prices have remained stable for the ten years, and national income has shown a steady growth. The rise in consumer prices is rather moderate; lower than in France and Britain and higher than in W. Germany. The gap between wholesale and consumer prices is seen similarly with other countries, but its degree is relatively small. Incomes by industries for 1960 is as follows:

Agriculture, forestry & fishery 17%	Mining 1%
Manufacturing 32%	Construction 7%
Transportation & communication ... 7%	Commerce............9%
Administration & professional 27%	

Clearly manufacturing is the main pillar of growth. Correlations between productivity, real wages and employment are figured in Chart 6. Similarly with France, the rate of productivity rise is enormously high, leaving those of real wages and employ-

Table VI.   Relevant Economic Indicators for Italy

	Industrial Production Index	Employment Index	Productivity	Nominal Wage Index (hourly)	Wholesale Price Index	Real Wage Index	Consumer Price Index	National Income (million lire)	Growth of National Income
1953	100	100	100	100	100	100	100		
1954	109	102	107	103	99	104	103	11,880	
1955	120	103	116.5	107	100	107	105	12,995	9.4%
1956	128	105	122	113	101.7	111	108.8	13,939	7.3
1957	137	107	128	117	102.7	114	110.2	14,962	7.3
1958	142	105	135	123	100.9	122	113.3	15,915	6.4
1959	158	105	150.5	125	97.9	127.5	112.8	17,477	9.8
1960	180	112	160.5	129	98.8	130.5	115.4	19,078	9.7
1961	200	(119)*	168	134	99.0	135.5	117.8	20,975	10.0
1962	220			145	102.0	142.0	123.5		

Note; data on dividend income are unavailable because they are not reported to the United Nations.
(*denotes figure for June, 1961.)

ment behind.   Indices of industrial production by sections for 1961 show high rate rises (base year 1963); for chemical fibres 326%, chemicals 273%, transport equipment 256%, oil refining 256%, metals 248%, and ceramics 224%.   In contrast, slower growth is seen for; textiles 126%, woods 152%, tobacco 138% and food 159%.   Herein we can find the cause for rising productivity, based on the levelling-up of industrial structures and prolongation of roundabout production.   However, due to the high rate of growth, the substitution between labor and capital is not so explicitly manifested as in America.

Among wholesale prices by groups, those with high rate for 1953–61 are; culture and amusement expenditures of 146% and transportation charges of 135.3%.   Low rates are for auto & bicycle 95.3% and electricity & gas 99.8%.   Food with 113.8% is also a little lower than the average.   Rises in labor and service and decline in capital service are clearly presented.   Agricultural production showed smooth growth, with a 48 per cent rise for 1958–61.

Chart 6.

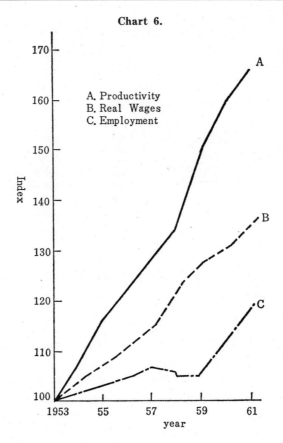

A. Productivity
B. Real Wages
C. Employment

VII. West Germany

Situations in W. Germany are somewhat different from those
in France and Italy. The growth rate of nominal national income is substantially the same with that in France, as seen in
Table VII. A slight rise in wholesale prices is seen, but not so
significant. The growth is steady with smaller inflationary effects as compared with France. Also the rate of consumer price
rise is relatively low. Thus far positions resemble those in Italy.
Incomes by industries for 1960 are:

Agriculture, forestry & fishery 7%

> Mining & manufacturing 52%
> Transportation & commerce............................20%
> Administration & professional.........................21%

The weight of manufacturing is high samely with, or higher than,
other European countries. However, the correlations between
productivity, real wages and employment, as shown in Chart 7,
are of inflationary trend, more clearly than in Britain in Chart 3.
Then, is the germ of mechanization for raising productivity emerging? In the production indices for 1961 high rates are found
for investment goods of 365% (base year 1950) and basic materials of 275%, while low rates for mining with 150% and
consumer goods with 220%. Herein a tendency toward prolonged
roundabout production is clear. Nevertheless the rise in productivity has not been catching up with those in real wages and
employment, because, for one thing, the substitution between
capital and labor does not explicitly present itself because of
the high rate growth. Another explanation may be that the
real wages in the base year 1953 were too low. To prove this
explanation, we must make international comparison of real wages
and productivity for 1953, or measure the Douglas production
function of the time. If the wages were not low at the base

Table VII. Relevant Economic Indicators for W. Germany

	Industrial Production Index	Employment Index	Productivity	Hourly Wages (Mark)	Wholesale Price Index	Real Wage Index	Consumer Price Index
1953	100	100	100	1.63	100.0	100	100.0
1954	112	105	107	1.67	98.4	104	100.1
1955	129	113	114	1.78	100.1	109	101.7
1956	139	121	115	1.94	101.5	117	104.4
1957	147	126	117	2.17	103.4	129	106.5
1958	152	128	119	2.32	103.0	138	108.8
1959	162	131	124	2.44	102.2	147	109.9
1960	179	134	133	2.68	103.4	159	111.4
1961	191	142	135	2.96	104.9	173	114.3
1962	200			3.30	106.0	185	118.3

	National Income (billion Mark)	Growth of National Income	Share of Earned Income	Farm Population (1000 persons)	Commercial Population (1000 persons)	Agricultural Production Index	Retail Sales Index
1953	110.6		59.2	970.8	1,603.7	100	
1954	119.7	8.3	60.2	925.3	1,733.3	101	100
1955	137.5	14.9	59.6	879.6	1,880.7	102	110
1956	152.1	10.9	60.5	862.9	2,059.3	102	120
1957	165.8	9.0	60.7	873.6	2,235.1	102	
1958	177.5	7.1	61.4	771.2	2,339.8	109	130
1959	192.2	8.3	61.7	768.5	2,466.3	121.5	135
1960	220.2*	11.0	60.7	657.0	2,663.3	130	146
1961	240.8	9.4	62.2	584.1	2,777.0	160	156
1962	260.2	8.1	64.0	531.5	2,920.7	179.5	163

(*Below Saar is included.)

Chart 7.

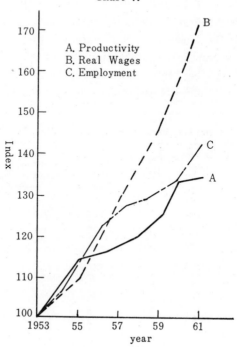

A. Productivity
B. Real Wages
C. Employment

time, we must say mechanization has been delayed due to insufficient capital accumulation, despite of appreciable differentials in the production indices by industrial sections. It is problematic to say, however, that this means a resemblance to British type. In view of significant changes in industrial structures, factual analysis about each particular section may be necessary.

Employment in commerce (including finance, hence, with fear of some error) and volume index of retail sales, as shown in Table VII, reveal that the per-employee sales volume is almost un-changed either for 1958–61 or for 1954–61, and so it is impossible to say higher efficiency in commerce has worked to prevent the rises in consumer prices. Among consumer price indices by groups for 1961 (base year 1958) high rates are for housing of 118.0% and culture and amusement expenditures of 108.7%, and low rates for drinks and tobacco of 99.0% and furnitures with 101.1%. Here, rises in service prices and shortage of housing are apparent, as in other European countries. It should be noted that, samely as is in Japan, the price of vegetables marked 145 per cent in 1961 (base year 1950), the highest among retail prices registering mean value of 115. As Table VII shows, farm population has declined drastically, and the index of labor productivity has recorded steep rises to 154 for 1958 and 266 for 1961. The stable vegetable price for 1958–61 may be explained by this high productivity, but general situations before this period remain questionable. For, agricultural prices cannot be explained solely by productivity, still more in view of the stable consumer prices lacking in productivity increase (our analysis is incomplete because data on agricultural wages are unavailable). Anyhow, a further detailed study is necessary for German economy.

VIII. Japanese Economic Situation

It is generally said that the Japanese economy is making a miraculous growth. The growth rates of nominal national income for recent five years are; 4.5% for 1958, 16.8% for 1959, 13.2% for 1960, 16.0% for 1961 and 10.5% (estimate) for 1962.

The average for the years is 12.2%, being a high one compared
with other countries, even when the 20 per cent rise in consumer
prices is taken into account. Hence, the problem facing present
Japan is not such "aggregate" one as stagnation, but one concerning the structural change, particularly the limping trend
between wholesale and retail prices. During the period 1953–62
the volume of manufacturing production has increased 3.47-fold
and the level of employment 2-fold. The rise in labor productivity is 79 per cent, and that of real wages 84 per cent. These
relations are indicated in Table VIII and Chart 8. In the mean-
time manufacturing has raised its share in national income from
24.3 per cent in 1953 to 29.8 per cent in 1962. However, the rise
in productivity is behind that in real wages, as seen in the Chart.
For such a phenomenon an advance of mechanization is thinkable,
but employment also has realized a very high rate of growth.
Two reasons for this are supposable. First, due to the extremely
speedy growth of manufacturing production, mechanization, if
any, did not require standstill or decline in employment. Second,
the rise in productivity was hampered by the attitude of enterprises that had to stick to the traditional labor-intensive production partly due to the difficulty of raising money, although ap-

Table VIII. Relevant Economic Indicators for Japan's Agriculture

	Agricultural Production Index	Labor Force (1000 persons)	Daily Wages* (yen)	Rural Price Index	Productivity	Real Wages
1953	93.4	14,560	264	108.7	72.5	81.4
1954	102.9	13,580	292	105.2	85.6	93.0
1955	124.5	14,090	301	100.7	100.0	100.0
1956	117.4	13,310	311	98.4	100.0	106.0
1957	122.1	13,760	326	100.0	100.0	109.0
1958	127.2	12,770	340	96.7	112.7	117.5
1959	130.6	12,040	351	98.5	122.5	119.0
1960	133.3	11,880	382	104.0	126.7	118.3
1961	134.6	11,460	466	113.1	132.5	137.7
1962	135.4*	11,570*	552.5	115.8	132.1	160.0

* Preliminary (daily pay for male worker)

Manufacturing

	Production Index	Employ- ment Index	Produc- tivity	Nominal Wage Index	Wholesale Price Index	Real Wage Index
1953	37.3	58.4	62.0	67.2	99.8	67.3
1954	39.8	61.5	64.5	70.8	99.2	71.5
1955	43.0	63.5	67.7	73.6	97.5	75.5
1956	53.0	69.5	76.3	80.4	101.7	79.2
1957	63.0	78.0	80.7	83.2	105.0	79.2
1958	63.2	79.7	79.0	85.5	97.8	87.5
1959	79.6	86.5	92.0	92.6	98.8	92.8
1960	100.0	100.0	100.0	100.0	100.0	100.0
1961	119.9	110.7	108.3	111.9	101.0	110.5
1962	129.1	116.8	111.0	123.0	99.3	124.0

Chart 8.

A. Productivity
B. Real Wages
C. Employment

parently mechanization would bring about cost reduction. This might be a transitional phenomenon, but in a sense resembles the situations in Britain.

These facts in manufacturing, i.e. increasing labor demand—

progress of mechanization—growing labor mobility, have worked influences on other industries. In agriculture, farm labor population began to decline with 1957, being most remarkable in 1958-9 and thereafter stagnant. It seems, the labor outflow to manufacturing reached a pause then, but at the same time, daily wages of farm labor turned to steep rise. Farm real wages rose by 35 per cent during 1959-61, although agricultural prices also showed some increase. As the rise in productivity was about 7 per cent, the gap between productivity and real wages was wider than in the case of manufacturing, resulting in the rise in agricultural prices. In contrast to total wholesale prices remaining at crablike positions for the three years, a 17 per cent rise was recorded for agricultural products, particularly for vegetables. The basic reason for such rise lies in the said wide gap between real wages and productivity, requiring modernization in agriculture for its cure. It must be noted, however, that such gap was not one bringing hardship to farm households as enterprise. Surplus income of farm households increased: 25,534 yen in 1958, 32,359 yen in 1959, 44,573 yen in 1960, 50,283 yen in 1961. Farm consumption level also rose by 22.8 per cent in real terms for 1959-62. This trend will continue as long as the expansion of effective demand, particularly that for dairy products, is sustained following the increase in national income.

IX. The Splendid Growth in Japan

Recently the problem of increasing distribution cost is earnestly discussed. It has been raised from the faster rise in consumer prices as against wholesale prices, the former registering 12 per cent for 1960-62 while the latter being constant. In the background of this phenomenon a problem of changing cost structure, in other words the westernization of cost structure, accompanying capital accumulation, is involved, say, "dear consumer goods and cheap producer goods." We shall first take up the cost in distribution. As adequate indices of volume of commercial sales are not available, we must use per-employee

Table IX. Data on Commerce in Japan

	Nominal Commercial Income (billion yen)	Retail Price Index	Real Commercial Income	Commercial Population (1000 persons)	Per-Employee Real Income
1952	832	100.0	832	6,010	138.5
1953	912	103.5	880	6,510	135.0
1954	963	106.9	900	7,510	120.0
1955	1,065	102.4	1,040	7,330	142.0
1956	1,234	102.1	1,210	7,940	152.5
1957	1,302	104.4	1,245	7,680	156.0
1958	1,334	103.2	1,295	8,320	155.5
1959	1,604	102.9	1,330	8,490	156.5
1960	1,926	105.7	1,820	9,000	202.0
1961	2,220	110.9	2,000	8,710	229.5
1962		115.2		8,990	229.0

real income as the index of productivity. As for 1962, however, the national income figures are not yet publicated, so we rely on the data of change in sales volume 1961 to 62 for computing productivity, assuming that the shares remain unchanged. The figures on employment in Table IX include finance and estate business employees, since they are not specified in the survey of labor force. This implicitly assumes parallel movements between finance-estate employees and wholesale-retail trade employees. Contrastively to farm population, commercial population has shown no marked decrease, although it began to decline since 1960 after steady increases in preceding years. Productivity rose sharply in 1950–60, but was stagnant for 1961–62. On the other hand, wages moved as follows:

	Nominal wages	Real wages
1959	21,457 yen	20,850 yen
1960	23,139	21,900
1961	24,144	25,300
1962	26,907	32,100

(monthly wages)

Real wages as cost have recorded a sharp rise in 1961–62, and resulted in the consumer price rise side by side with the stagnant

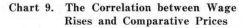

Chart 9. The Correlation between Wage
Rises and Comparative Prices

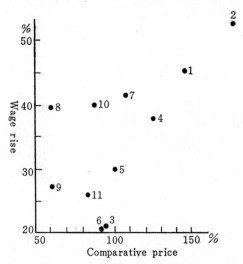

productivity. To solve the problem a decrease in employment by
way of capital-intensive method of trading may be necessary.

To speak from classical view, the value of labor rises with
economic growth, and naturally prices in capital-intensive industries decline relatively more. Next, we shall positively examine the "westernization of price structure" and its effects
upon employment and wages.

In the case of Japan, the most weighty effect of trade liberalization will come from the relation with American economy.
Prices of principal commodities in both countries as for the
summer of 1961 are compared in Table X. The comparative
prices there are obtained by dividing export prices in America
(after converting into yen prices) by domestic market prices in
Japan and then multiplying the results 100-fold. If a relative
price is over 100, Japan's ware is cheaper. On the other hand,
the multiple rates of wages in the Table are computed by dividing
average wages in American industrial sections (in U.S. Department of Labor; Employment and Earnings, Sept., 1959) by those

Table X.   US-Japan Comparative Prices and Wages

Comparative Price		Industry	Multiple Rate of Wages	Change (Japan) 1959–61	1959–62
Cotton yarn	144	1. Textile manufact.	6,580	26.4%	45.5%
Cotton fabric	111	2. Fabric manufact.	7,492	30.0	52.5
Rayon yarn	173				
Staple fibre	227				
Pig iron	97.5	3. Primary metal manufact.	5,384	17.2 (steel)	21.0
Steel bar	117.0				
Steel plate	90.8				
Steel thin plate	75.9				
Electro-copper	87.0			19.5	26.5
Electro-lead	98.4			(non-ferrous metals)	
Electro-zinc	86.5				
Tin	97.4				
Aluminium	100.5				
Cement	125	4. Stone & glass manufact.	6,778	22.1	38.0
Ammonium sulfate	112.3	5. Chemicals	6,458	19.2	30.0
Caustic soda	97.4				
Rayon pulp	89.0	6. Paper manufact.	6,258	11.2	20.5
Bean oil	92.5				
Crude rubber	106	7. Rubber manufact.	10,010	25.0	41.5
Cowhide	59.0	8. Leather manufact.	4,483	24.4	39.5
Coal	60.2	9. Mining	5,657	16.7	27.0
Heavy oil	86.5	10. Oil & coal manufact.	6,566	31.2	40.0

in Japan (in Ministry of Labor; Monthly Labor Statistics).   On the Table, the Spearman's coefficient of rank correlation becomes 0.734, representing some degree of correlation (putting aside the smallness of sample).   Hence, we could say "wages are relatively low in those industries with relatively low prices of products".

In Chart 9 is illustrated the correlation between the rates of wage increase for 1959–62 and the comparative prices, as computed in Table X.   (As to those industries with several sorts of products, e.g. steel, mean value of such several prices, or where even numbers simple arithmetic average of median two values, is taken as the comparative price.)   By the Chart we could broadly say that high rate of wage increase is recognized for those industrial sections with relatively low comparative price, excepting an extreme case of leather manufacturing. This seems to tell that, with economic growth, even under condition of closed economy the price structure tends to shift toward patterns of advanced countries, and, in addition, the trade liberalization has worked to smooth the unevenness in the price structure. This finding will serve as an useful material for observing the future of price and wage structures in Japan.

X. The Rise of Consumer Prices in Japan

Then, in our economy, how are the correlations between productivity, wages and employment? Table XI reveals the changes in these three items during 1959–62. This is just the period when, against the background of "Iwato boom", such problems as labor shortage, changes in price structure, and the shift to Western type of economy were arising. In the Table, productivity indices by industrial (median) sections are computed from the index of industrial production by the Ministry of International Trade and Industry, the index of agricultural production by the Ministry of Agriculture and Forestry, and above cited data on real income of retail trade.

First, employment and nominal wages are in non-correlation on the whole, as seen in Chart 10. While in America employment decreased or showed crablike trends, and the substitution between labor and capital emerged in industries with high rate of wage increase, in the case of Japan such phenomena are not discernible. This seems to depend on the facts that industries were feeling the need of reserving labor power amid the mood of high tempo growth, and that the period was still a transitional stage toward capital-intensive production. However, a move toward prolonged roundabout production is recognizable by the highest growth of machinery manufacturing and the lowest one

Table XI.   Changes in Wages, Production, Employment and Productivity in Japan, 1959 to 1962

Industry	Wages	Production	Employment	Productivity
1. Mining	127.0%	119.0%	79.8%	136.5%
2. Construction	143.0		187.0	
3. Food manufact.	132.5	121.5	150.7	80.8
4. Tobacco	134.0	129.5	111.0	104.0
5. Textiles	145.5	117.3	111.5	105.2
6. Clothes & belongings	152.5	117.0	132.0	89.7
7. Sawing	140.5	121.0	100.8	120.0
8. Furnitures	147.5		136.5	
9. Paper	120.5	142.0	121.5	117.0
10. Publishing & printing	138.3		118.0	
11. Chemicals	119.2	154.0	125.5	123.0
12. Oil & coal	140.0	172.5	106.0	162.7
13. Rubber	141.5	158.0	128.0	123.3
14. Hide & leather	139.5	173.3	135.0	128.3
15. Ceramics & stone	138.0	160.0	131.0	122.0
16. Iron & steel	121.0	164.5	174.5	94.5
17. Non-ferrous metals	126.5	155.5	134.0	116.0
18. Metal products	136.0		152.5	
19. Machinery	129.0	201.0	160.0	111.5
20. Electrical equip.	118.0	207.0	164.0	126.0
21. Transport equip.	122.0	192.5	142.5	135.0
22. Precision instruments	140.0	186.5	135.3	137.0
23. Miscellaneous manufact.	148.5	174.0	129.0	135.0
24. Wholesale & retail trade	125.0		147.3	146.0
25. Finance & insurance	127.0		129.7	
26. Real estates	133.0		105.0	
27. Transport & communication	134.0		120.0	
28. Gas & electricity	131.5	146.5	110.0	133.3
29. Agriculture	157.5			108.0

for textile section. It is noteworthy also that, with a shift to Western type of price structure, the growth rate in light industries, particularly intextiles, would slow down due to relative rise in wages, while that of heavy industries would be relatively

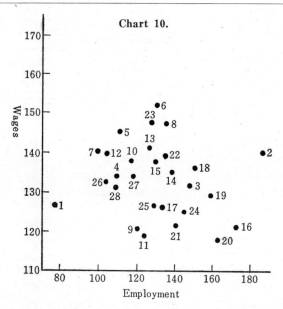

Chart 10.

accelerated. A germ pointing to such trend could be found in the facts that metals and machinery sections have low rate of wage increase and high rate of employment increase while textile section has high rate of wage increase and low rate of employment increase. The low increase rates of wages and employment in mining and the vise-versa in construction depend obviously on the respective trends of effective demand. As for mining, the high comparative prices of Japan's mining products are making a reason for stagnant effective demand, and so employment in this industry would have been in a higher level under the condition of closed economy.

The correlation between the rate of productivity rise and that of wage rise is seen in Chart 11. Equality between two rates is recognized only for (28) gas & electricity and near equality for (22) precision instruments. High wage increase, compared with productivity rise, is seen for (29) agriculture, (6) clothes & belongings, (23) miscellaneous manufacturing and (5) textiles. The reason why the price of textile goods, despite of such high rate of wage increase, remained at moderate rise, i.e. 9 per cent

for consumer price and 6 per cent for wholesale price in 1960–
62, may be found in the condition that the demand for these
goods has small income elasticity and large price elasticity.
Some agricultural products other than staple food, with large
income elasticity and small price elasticity, showed price rise.
Conversely, (12) oil & coal is a section with low rate of wage
increase relative to productivity rise. The wholesale price of
this section marked a 7.5 per cent drop for 1960–62. A problematic case is (24) wholesale & retail trade whose relative "price",
distribution cost, increased. This may have been derived from the
scarce rise in productivity and some rise in wages.

Chart 11.

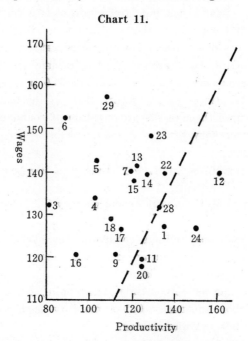

On the ground of the above observation we could say:
(1) In the Japanese economy after the "Iwato boom", being
faced with labor shortage, the behavior of the supply side of
labor has been strongly imposed on the wage decision, whereas
the position of demand side, intending to provide the fruit of

productivity rise for improving real wages and employment, has not been so clearly represented.

(2) The substitution between labor and capital, to follow wage increase, is not yet explicit. This resembles the situation in Britain. But in view of the emerging structural changes in industry, the substitution is expected to arise sooner or later.

(3) The prolongation of roundabout production will be unavoidably accelerated by the economic growth as well by the trade liberalization.

The share of earned income in the nation's national income had been on a gradual increase with the rise in production level in the early postwar years, but later changed to a declining trend with 1958 of 52.4 per cent as the turning point, being 51.0 per cent in 1951. This is due to the increasing corporate income by buoyant business, but the share of earned income is still low, as compared internationally. It has risen to 53.0 per cent in 1962, but for a further increase an upward shift of the marginal labor productivity curve through the prolongation of roundabout production will be necessary.

XI. US-Japan Comparative Prices and Wages

Though our analysis is very crude, we may tentatively conclude as below.

First, our previous findings regarding the period about 1950, as abridged in the beginning section of this paper, requires revision on one point; that is:

(1) Now Japan as well as Italy are stepping into the economic pattern of labor shortage. Labor mobility is increasing and wage differentials are diminishing.

And, our new findings are:

(2) Böhm-Wicksell's theory on roundabout production holds true to advanced countries also, when the growth rate is low or fluctuates with a wide breadth.

(3) The share of labor in a nation's income depends on the absolute level of labor productivity. The existence or non-ex-

istence of cost inflation has no direct relation with the share but works effect on its stability.

(4)   The increasing distribution cost is a phenomenon common to all countries, causing the gap between consumer and whole-sale prices.   The tempo of increase in distribution cost seems to be affected by the rise in the productivity in commerce, excepting the case in Germany where such explanation is not complete.   The rise in agricultural prices is especially remarkable for Japan, which may have a certain degree of relation with the increase in productivity (in a relative sense with the increase in agricul-tural wages).

(5)   The fundamental cause for inflation or non-inflation lies in the existence or non-existence of bottle-necks, but the pace of inflation may have a relation with the relative speed of rises between productivity and wages.

(6)   Cost inflation has no relationship with the high-or-low of economic growth, but relationship with the rise-or-non-rise in productivity by mechanization conforming to the increase in real wages.   Mechanization is not yet complete in Japan, Britain and Germany, suggesting insufficient capital accumulation.

(7)   Explanation by the demand function of labor is applicable to America, France and Italy.   In Japan, Britain and Germany the supply side of labor appears to have worked more strongly on wage decision.

(8)   In the case of Japan, the westernization of price and wage structures will be promoted by both factors of internal economic growth and external trade liberalization.   However, after passing a transitional phase, average prices would not rise so remarkably, if cost-down by mechanization were realized.